# THE IROQUOIS

# THE IROQUOIS

## A HISTORY OF THE SIX NATIONS

## OF NEW YORK

BY

## S. C. KIMM, A. M., Ph. D.

SUPERVISING PRINCIPAL OF THE MIDDLEBURGH SCHOOLS

MIDDLEBURGH, N. Y.

———— ——— o——— ————

"It was the foe, fierce, brave and strong,
Who for your homes contending stood,
That brought the need which wrought ere long
Your mighty league of brotherhood.
And though it only lives in name,
Or on the bold historic page,
O keep its bright, proud hero-fame
Unsullied still from age to age."
*Hathaway.*

———— ——— o——— ————

MIDDLEBURGH, N. Y.
PRESS OF PIERRE W. DANFORTH
1900

THIS PUBLICATION IS A
FACSIMILE REPRINT
OF THE ORIGINAL BOOK

Published by

J. C. & A. L. Fawcett, Inc.
38-01 23rd Avenue
Astoria, NY 11105

Published in the United States

ISBN 0-941567-42-7

# INTRODUCTION

The author's object in presenting to the public this short History of the Six Nations is to place in complete form the material, gathered here and there, often from sources not available to the general reader, necessary to an understanding of the lives and motives of the people who composed that powerful confederacy which controlled for many years the polity of all the tribes living in the limits of what is now the North Central States of our country. Statesmen by nature, and conquerors by practice, they were well named the "Romans of the West." And although they stood as a strong bulwark between the French and Dutch, and later between the French and English and thus were largely influential in preserving their hunting grounds for the Anglo-Saxon race, yet slight mention is made of them in our school histories, and little opportunity is given our boys and girls to learn what an important part they played in the early history of our colonial and national life. Had they thrown their influence on the side of the French there is every reason to believe that this country, which to-day offers the greatest opportunities for the development of the human race, would not be under the rule of the descendants of the liberty loving Teutons. If this little volume should serve in some small degree to keep green the memory of an unfortunate people, who seemed by nature destined for greater things, then its mission will have been accomplished.

The author wishes to take this opportunity to thank
the Rev. George Hardy, of Sauquoit, N. Y., for his
timely article on the Oneida Indians, and to Hon. G.
L. Danforth, A. M., Hon. J. Edward Young, Mr.
John Mallery and others for access to their excellent
private libraries.

———

## REFERENCES

McMaster's United States History.
Parkman's Historical Works.
Robert's New York State History.
Fisk's Discovery of America.
New York Civil List.
Beauchamp's New York State Museum.
The Annals of America.
Smith's History of New York.
Morgan's League of the Iroquois.
Schoolcraft's Notes on the Iroquois.
The Iroquois, by Minnie Myrtle.
Documentary History of New York.
Simm's Border Warfare.
Dr. Colden's History of the Five Nations.
Stone's Life of Brant.
Campbell's Border Wars of New York.
Lossing's Empire State.

# THE IROQUOIS

## CHAPTER I

### THE SIX NATIONS

The first European who touched American shores found here a race of human beings unlike any that he had ever come in contact with before. On the shores of the stormy Atlantic, the smiling Pacific, in the frozen North, beneath the scorching rays of the torrid sun, and on the snow clad peaks of the mighty Andes, were found the same race, characterized by copper colored complexion, high cheek bones, straight black hair, and small deep set eyes. Whence came this race covering such a vast territory, and ranging in culture from the lowest grade of savagery up to the highest grade of barbarism? It is not the province of this paper to discuss the origin of man, nor to attempt to prove either that Adam was the ancestor of the human family, or, as many scientists think, that man appeared in various parts of the earth contemporaneous with the biblical Adam. Before men took up the study of Geology it was supposed that there had been no great changes in the form of the land masses of the earth, and so the relations of the continents of America and Asia had remained the same since the advent of man. Because Europeans had never come in contact with such a race before, they concluded that in some remote age he must have come from Asia or some Asiatic islands, and so many theories have been advanced showing how they first reached these shores. Bancroft, speaking of their origin and consanguinity, says, "Schoolmen and scientists count their theories by the hundreds, each sustaining some pet conjecture with a logical clearness equalled only by the facility with which he demolishes all the rest. One proves their origin by Holy writ, another by the sage sayings of the fathers. One discovers in them Phoenician merchants, another the ten lost tribes of Israel. They are tracked with equal certainty from Scandinavia, from Ireland, from Iceland, from Greenland, across Behring Strait, across the Northern Pacific, the Southern Pacific, from the Polynesian Islands, from Australia, from Africa. Venturesome Carthagenians were thrown upon the eastern shore, Japanese junks on the western. The breezes that wafted hither America's primogenitors are still blowing, and the ocean currents by which they came cease not yet to flow. The finely spun webs of logic by which these fancies are maintained would prove amusing did not the profound earnestness of their respective advocates render them ridiculous."

The more we study the American Indian, from the light of geology and ethnological history, the more we are of the opinion that the Autochthonic theory of the origin of our aborigines is the most in accord with recent discoveries and consequently the most satisfactory of acceptance. In the first place had he emigrated from Asia he would have had the same blood in his veins that coursed through the veins of those Asiatics who founded the Ancient Eastern Civilizations. If such were the case, how was it that he remained in a state of primeval savagery so many centuries while his brethern were developing such a high state of civilization in the parent country ? Blood will tell ! With all the natural advantages which the American continent offers, scarcely equaled anywhere in the world, one would expect as rapid development in civilization on the American continent as in Asia. But such was not the case. Nowhere has there ever been discovered any remains that showed much knowledge of art or science. People who had intelligence enough to construct ships or other means of transporting themselves across so great distances would have had intelligence enough to have preserved some memorial of so great an event. But proofs of such are entirely wanting. Their traditions and myths go back to their creation, and yet it is to be strongly questioned whether there is much similarity between them and those of Eastern continents—enough to even partially prove a common origin. The fact that they had many social customs, habits and religious rites similar to other people's in a savage state proves nothing beyond the fact that all men in the same plane of savagery and barbarism have exhibited the same mental, moral and physical traits.

Whatever theory may be adopted as to their origin, or whatever birth place may be assigned them, this one thing all men are agreed upon, the American aborigines have occupied this continent during a much greater period than was formerly thought. Traditions, earth mounds, moral and physical peculiarities prove this. And yet when we contemplate that each successive age has left no more track upon the waste of time than a ship leaves in crossing the ever changing deep there is seen something of the difficulties to be overcome in arriving at some definite knowledge concerning the primitive Indian. Bryant says in his noble poem, "Thanatopsis," "All that tread the globe, are but a handful to the tribes that slumber in its bosom." Science is coming to our aid and the hand of genius may yet gradually lead us back through at least part of the long, dark, silent past into the realm of the primeval Indian where may be revealed to us his early, physical characteristics.

Researches during the last fifty years have already thrown much light on the ethnology of the American savage. Shell mounds of great antiquity have been found on the banks of the St. John's, Alabama, and Mississippi Rivers, and in many other localities. The glacial period was the most characteristic of the Pleiocene age which occurred certainly more than 50,000 years ago. Traces of the existence of human beings in North America during the glacial period have been found in abundance. Quartzite implements have been found in the drift near the city of St. Paul. A part of a human jaw was discovered in a deposit of red clay belonging to the early part of the glacial period. Over sixty implements, three human skulls and other bones were found securely imbedded in the Trenton gravel. Discoveries by Prof. Winchell show that in all probability all the continent from the Atlantic to the Mississippi river was inhabited by this race during the great ice age. In 1866 a human skull was discovered in the gold bearing gravels of the Pleiocene age. This discovery has called forth many heated arguments and learned disquisitions from scientific men. What makes the discovery so interesting is the fact that the fossil remains of two apes most nearly like man in physical structure were found in the Upper Miocene. By the agitation one would think that these learned men are afraid that Darwin's "Missing Link" may yet be found.

In entering upon the study of the people found upon this continent by Europeans that which strikes us most forcibly is the great number of languages spoken by the different tribes. Squier put the number at 400 while Ludewig claimed there were 1,100. These languages were divided into several thousand dialects. This proves that there was a sparse population consisting of many scattered tribes. About the eleventh or twelfth century there existed east of the Mississippi River three great families. One of these, the Algon-

quins, occupied all that region east of the Great Lakes
as far north as Hudson's Bay and east to Labrador.
This family was divided into many tribes the names of
which frequently occur in the writings of the colonists,
and novelists, like Cooper. About the thirteenth or
fourteenth century an offshoot of the great Dakota
family known in history as the Huron–Iroquois family
seem to have moved eastward, something as did the
hordes from the great German forests in early European history. They, like the Teutons, were the most
hardy and aggressive men on the continent. Tho'
numbering far less than their neighbors they pushed
their way eastward to Niagara where they separated,
part working their way up the St. Lawrence and another part going down the Susquehanna. The Hurons settled in the peninsula between the Great
Lakes. Another part afterward known as "The Neutral Nation" settled near Lake Erie. The Susquehan-
nocks, in the fertile valley of a great river which is
called after them to-day, while the Tuscaroras went as
far south as North Carolina. The group which moved
along the north bank of the St. Lawrence were perhaps the most hardy and the most intelligent and important of all the aborigines north of the Gulf of Mex-
ico. Cortes in 1536 found one of their villages
"beautiful for situation" on the present site of Montreal. But they seem to have been driven out by the
vastly greater numbers of the Algonquins, for several
years later when Champlain visited the country the
beautiful Iroquois village had vanished. Doubtless
the larger part of them moved across the river and
lake to a locality near the present site of Oswego,
where the three small but fearless tribes of the Iroquois
established themselves. At first they consisted of the
Senecas, Mohawks and Onondagas, but afterward two
of these tribes became divided forming two additional

tribes, viz., the Cayugas and Oneidas. Just when these five tribes united to form that great "Barbaric Republic" which played such an interesting part in the intercolonial wars, is not certainly known, but it must have occurred previous to the discovery of America by Columbus.

# CHAPTER II

THE Iroquois have a very pretty legend relating to their origin and final union into a confederacy. A great many years ago they were confined under a mountain near the falls of the Oswego from where they were led by the "Holder of the Heavens" into the beautiful Mohawk valley, along which and farther westward they settled, each tribe in a different locality. About this time the sixth tribe, known as the Tuscaroras, left and moved toward where the birds fly in winter. The remaining five tribes kept up a continual warfare with one another. After a time a fierce and warlike tribe came from the home of the north wind and falling upon the Onondagas nearly exterminated them. This threw the Iroquois tribes into the greatest consternation. Unless they could overcome these northern barbarians their whole nation would perish. In their great distress they called upon the "Holder of the.Heavens," affectionately called by the people Hi-a-wat-ha "The Very Wise Man." The Iroquois were his dearest children so they followed his advice at all times. Hi-a-wat-ha told them to call representatives from all the tribes to a great council to be held on the banks of Onondaga Lake. The great council fire blazed for three days and yet no Hi-a-wat-ha appeared to help or to advise. At length guided by the Great Spirit he was seen coming across the lake in a white canoe bearing with him his beautiful little daughter. Scarcely had they landed upon the shore when there suddenly arose a mighty wind and an immense bird so large as to darken the landscape swooped down upon the beautiful girl and crushed her into the earth. Speechless with grief Hi-a-wat-ha mourned for his daughter three days. Then he said, "I will meet you to-morrow and unfold to you my plans." On the following day he arose in the council and spoke as follows :

"Brothers; you have come here from a great distance to provide safety for yourselves and your homes. How should it be done ? We can make no progress by opposing these tribes from the cold north singly. We must unite all our tribes into one band of brothers. In that way we shall be able to keep our enemies from our land."

"You, the Mohawks, sitting under the shadow of the 'Great Tree,' whose roots sink deep into the earth, and whose branches spread over a vast country, shall be the first nation, because you are warlike and mighty."

"And you, Oneidas, a people who recline your bodies against the 'Everlasting Stone,' that cannot be moved, shall be the second nation, because you give wise counsel."

"And you, Onondagas, who have your habitation at the 'Great Mountain' and are overshadowed by its crags, shall be the third nation, because you are gifted in speech, and are mighty in war."

"And you, Cayugas, whose habitation is the 'Dark Forest,' and whose home is everywhere, shall be the fourth nation, because of your superior cunning in hunting."

"And you, Senecas, a people who live in the 'Open Country,' and possess much wisdom, shall be the fifth nation, because you understand better the art of raising corn and beans, and making cabins."

"You, five great and powerful nations, must unite

and have but one common interest, and no foe shall be able to disturb or subdue you. If we unite, the Great Spirit will smile upon us. Brothers, these are the words of Hi-a-wat-ha; let them sink deep into your hearts. Admit no other nations, and you will always be free, numerous and happy. If other tribes and nations are admitted to your councils they will sow the seeds of jealousy and discord, and you will become few, feeble and enslaved. Remember these words. They are the last you will hear from Hi-a-wat-ha. The Great Master of Breath calls me to go. I have patiently awaited his summons. I am ready to go. Farewell!"

The legend tells us that when the good Hi-a-wat-ha finished his speech the air was filled with the sweetest music. The beautiful white canoe rose slowly into the air, and it bore their good friend and wise councillor far into the eternal blue. The music slowly died away and the dusky savages were left to try the experiment of becoming a confederated nation.

# CHAPTER III

THEY proudly called themselves Ongwe–Honwe, "Men all surpassing others," and it has been said that "They were the proudest representatives of natural manhood ever discovered." Strange as it may seem the white men who carried on negotiations with these sons of the forest received a diplomatic training that enabled them to place New York in a position among the colonies far beyond that to which her size entitled her. The Iroquois designated themselves as Ho-de-no-san-nee, "A people dwelling in a long house." According to another writer, they called their confederacy Ko-no-shi-oni—the "Long House." Their territory seems to have extended from that occupied by the "Neutrals" near Lake Erie up to and even beyond the Hudson River. The Senecas were placed in the western part of their territories as a defence against the fierce, western tribes. Afterward the Iroquois extended their conquest as far as the Mississippi river, and "it was solely on this conquest that the English based their claims to that territory as against the French at the opening of the French and Indian war, and it was in this way that New York came into possession of that vast section which she gave to the United states from which were carved Ohio, Indiana, Illinois, Michigan and Wisconsin." For this alone both our state and national governments owe a great debt to this barbaric republic.

The eastern gate of their territory was kept by the Mohawks, in many respects the ablest warriors among

all the aborigines of America. Near Lake Onondaga
where Hi-a-wat-ha appeared to them in his beautiful
canoe they kept their great council fire, the capital of
the confederacy. It was the duty of the Onondagas to
guard this fire, the general meeting place of the nation.

# CHAPTER IV

## THE GOVERNMENT OF THE IROQUOIS

CLASSICAL students are apt to look to foreign lands as the birth place of political institutions. Long before Europeans had set foot upon these shores, the Iroquois had marked out a form of government "of the whole, by the whole, for the benefit of the whole," almost a prototype of that great government which followed it, —the best, and freest the world has ever seen. Remembering that this people had not yet developed beyond the barbaric stage, we are astonished to find so much in their form of government of what we are wont to expect only in the highest civilization. They were surrounded by tribes not advanced beyond the highest stages of savagery or the first stages of barbarism. They had never come in contact with people as intelligent as themselves. The refining influences of Christianity had never penetrated their strongholds, and they had no universities greater than the studies of nature and their simple lives. How did it happen that there was such a striking resemblance between their clan and tribal governments and that of our old Teutonic ancestors back in the German forests nearly 2000 years before ? Why had they the spirit of the old Greek Amphictyonic Council ? Our answer is this : Like needs have brought about like conditions of society in various ages in widely separated parts of the earth. When first discovered the Iroquois were fast conquering or at least gaining an influence over all the surrounding tribes. Their plan was largely one of extermination and adoption rather than of conquest. If they spared a tribe it was to levy tribute, and woe to that tribe if it refused to acknowledge their sovereignty. Some see.n to think that if they had not been checked in their career by the coming of the whites they would have extended their empire over the greater part of North America. Their domain extended from the St. Lawrence and the Great Lakes on the North to the Carolinas on the South, and from the lordly Hudson on the East to where the Ohio mingles its peaceful waters with the Mississippi.

Although their confederation was purely Democratic in spirit, yet, ruling over so large a territory, they found it necessary to adopt the representative form. They were constrained at first to form a league of defense against the more numerous and hostile tribes by which they were surrounded. This union developed their natural aptitude for government, and necessity compelled them to keep it in active operation. In a short time instead of acting on the defensive they became the most aggressive warriors on the American continent. Like the political fathers who framed our present constitution they made a wide distribution of power.

Lossing gives the following division: "Each canton or nation was a distinct republic, independent of all others in relation to its domestic affairs, but each bound to the others of the league by ties of honor and general interest. Each canton had eight principal sachems, or civil magistrates, and several inferior sachems. The whole number of civil magistrates in the confederacy amounted to nearly two hundred. There were fifty hereditary sachems."

"Each canton, or nation was subdivided into clans or tribes, each clan having a heraldic insignia called totem. For this insignia one tribe would have the figure of a wolf; another of a bear; another of a deer; another of a tortoise and so on. By their totemic system they maintained a perfect tribal union.  After the European came, the sachem of the tribe affixed his totem, in the form of a rude representation of the animal that marked his tribe, to the documents he was required to sign, 'like an ancient monarch affixing his seal.' "

Fiske in his Discovery of America says "The confederacy had no Chief Sachem or Chief Magistrate." But Lossing says "The League had a President clothed with powers similar to those conferred on the Chief Magistrate of the United States.  He had authority to assemble a Congress of Representatives of the League.  He had a cabinet of six advisors, and in the Grand Council he was moderator."

### PUBLIC OFFICE

It was only by merit that public office could be secured, and public opinion was the only reward for years of active service.

The Onondaga tribe was honored by having the first President selected from among their wise men.  Tradition says this man was Ato-tar-ho who lived in a swamp surrounded by hissing serpents, and who ate and drank from dishes made from the skulls of those whom he had slain in battle.

Receiving no pay but that of public favor, these sachems became renowned for their prudence and sagacity.  All affairs of great importance were transacted in the general council at Onondaga, but in local affairs and in cases of pressing emergency each nation acted for itself.

In one thing the Iroquois were not unlike the Romans ; military power was stronger than the civil power and often overthrew the latter by deposing the sachems.  The military leaders received their authority from the people, receiving the title of Chief.  A military leader wishing to secure a band of followers organized a war dance, which was the recruiting station of the tribe. It was never necessary to resort to conscription to fill the ranks. But however strong the army might be, there was a third party which had the right to veto a declaration of war. This party was composed of the matrons of the long houses who could demand a cessation of war; nor was it any disgrace for the bravest chief to bury the hatchet at the command of the peace party. In this one thing, at least, the Iroquois were a step in advance of the most highly civilized nations of to-day, "woman was man's co-worker in legislation." Pre-eminent in their love of freedom they never made slaves of any, not even captives in war. These they either killed or adopted into their own tribes. Born diplomats they excelled many a modern master of diplomatic art in tact, self repression and political sagacity.

# CHAPTER V

ONE of the most interesting things in the study of these Indians is that of their manner of building their habitations or "Long Houses." I quote from Mr. Morgan's "House Life of the American Aborigines." "The long house was from fifty to eighty and sometimes one hundred feet long. It consisted of a strong frame of upright poles set in the ground, which was strengthened with horizontal poles attached with withes, and surmounted with a triangular, and in some cases with a round roof. It was covered over, both sides and roof, with long strips of elm bark tied to the frame with strings or splints. An external frame of poles for the sides and of rafters for the roof was then adjusted to hold the bark shingles between them, the two frames being tied together. The interior of the house was comparted [divided] at intervals of six or eight feet, leaving each chamber entirely open like a stall upon the passage way which passed through the centre of the house from end to end. At each end was a doorway covered with suspended skins. Between each four apartments, two on a side, was a fire pit in the centre of the hall, used in common by their occupants. Thus a house with five fires would contain twenty apartments and accommodate twenty families, unless some apartments were reserved for storage. They were warm, roomy, and tidily-kept habitations. Raised bunks were constructed around the walls of each apartment for beds. From the roof poles were suspended their strings of corn in the ear, braided by the husks, also strings of dried squashes

and pumpkins.  Spaces were contrived here and there
to store away their accumulations of provisions.  Each
house, as a rule, was occupied by related families, the
mothers and their children belonging to the same gens,
while their husbands and the fathers of the children
belonged to other gentes; consequently the gens or
clan of the mother largely predominated in the household.  Whatever was taken in the hunt or raised by
cultivation by any member of the household was for
the common benefit.  Provisions were made a common
stock within the household.  Besides the food, the domestic utensils, the rude implements of husbandry,
and the children belonged wholly to the gens or clan.''

IROQUOIS WOMEN

Marriage life among the Indians was somewhat different from that among the white people of our times.
Fiske in his most excellent work—The Discovery of
America, says: "When a young woman got married
she brought her husband home with her.  Though
henceforth an inmate of this household he remained
an alien to her clan.  If he proved lazy and failed to
do his share of the providing, woe be to him.  No
matter how many children, or whatever goods he
might have in the house, he might at any time be
ordered to pick up his blanket and budge; and after
such orders it would not be healthful for him to dis-
obey, the house would be to hot for him and unless
saved by the intercession of some aunt or grandmother
of his wife he must retreat to his own clan, or, as was
often done, go and start a new matrimonial alliance in
some other.  The female portion ruled the house.''
And yet the wife was the slave of her husband.  It
was she who generally dressed the skins from which
she made clothing for the family and often built the
wigwam.  She cultivated the soil with the rudest implements while her husband hunted and fished or went

upon the warpath. One writer has said that "These women, in keeping secrets and in being close-mouthed excel all the other women of the world. Rubens nor Titian could hardly equal them in the skill of coloring their robes, belts of wampum, or birch boxes in red, blue or yellow. They used quills of porcupines as their pencils, and selected for their colors the leaves and blossoms of plants, chiefly the forest sumac and the juice of berries."

### POTTERY

The Iroquois excelled many of the other Indians in the manufacture of fabrics and domestic utensils, which they often ornamented with taste and skill. One of the most ancient of their arts was that of pottery. In very old mounds are found earthern pots and pipes with curious ornamentation. Some of this ware is so firm as to admit of considerable polish. The material out of which they made their pottery was clay and quartz. According to Morgan, who was well versed in the domestic life of the Iroquois, their clay pipes were as hard as marble. They often ornamented their pipes with the picture of some animal. Another kind of pipe was carved out of soap-stone.

In Indian burial places are found earthen pots holding, perhaps, five or six quarts in which had been deposited food for the departed to sustain them while on their journey to the realm of the Great Spirit.

### EDGE TOOLS

Metal utensils seem to have been unknown among the Iroquois before the advent of the white man [Morgan.] They made rude knives and chisels of flint and hornstone. The tomahawk also was made of stone and was shaped not unlike the steel axe of the present day, except that, instead of an eye, a groove was hollowed out around the tomahawk in which a crotched or split stick was fastened with a thong or

withe. They also made a kind of stone gouge, con-
cave, by means of which they hollowed out hard
stones for mortars in which they ground their corn,
paint, barks and roots for medicines. It was only
with the greatest labor that an Indian could cut down
trees, and cut them into logs. Fire was applied at
the foot and as fast as the wood became charred the
coal was scraped away till, after a long time, the tree
was burned through and fell. In the same manner it
was burned through at regular distances to make logs.

### BARK BARRELS, AND TRAYS

Perhaps more convenient articles were made out of
the bark of trees than of any other material. Barrels
were made of the inside bark of the red elm. It was
arranged so that the grain ran around the barrel, and
carefully fastened up and down the side with thread
made of thin bark or hide. These had a bottom and
not infrequently a cover and were used as receptacles
for seeds, corn, beans, dried fruits, and the like. They
were very durable, often being retained in the family
for a hundred years. [Morgan.] A flat piece of inside
bark from some large tree was turned up at the ends
and sides, which were held in place both inside and
out by splints of some very strong wood. This made
a very convenient tray for many uses. In these were
mixed the various ingredients from which were made
their most civilized food.

### ROPES AND STRAPS

From bark were also made the rope and strap with
which they carried their burdens. Rawhide was often
used but does not seem to have been as serviceable as
those made from bark. The inside bark of the elm or
basswood was secured and boiled in ashes and water.
Then it was dried and separated into filaments, which
were braided into various kinds of rope. That made
from slippery-elm was very pliable and the most dur-

able. The burden strap used by the Indian women was often ornamented with porcupine quill-work. These displayed a skill in design and workmanship scarcely equalled by the women of any barbaric nation.

### MAPLE SUGAR

One of the Indian festivals is that instituted to the maple and is known as the Maple Dance. Whether the Indian learned from the white man how to make sugar or the white man learned from the Indian is uncertain. [Morgan.] At any rate, the Indian sap-tub was a unique and handy article surpassing the trough used so many years by our forefathers. "A strip of bark about three feet in length by two in width, makes the tub. The rough bark is left upon the bottom and sides. At the joint where the bark is to be turned up to form the ends, the outer bark is removed; the inner rind is then turned up, gathered together in small folds at the top and tied around with a splint. It is then ready for use, and will last several seasons. Aside from the natural fact that the sap would be quite at home in the bark tub, and its flavor preserved untainted, it is more durable and capacious than the wooden one and more readily made." [Morgan.]

### THE BIRCH BARK CANOE.

The Indian also excelled in making his bark canoe which was, perhaps, his only conveyance worthy the name. It was so light that he could carry it around falls and obstructions, so strong that it could carry several tons, and, with good care and usage, would last many years. It was made from the bark of the birch, red-elm or hickory. A single piece of bark was taken from a tree from ten to forty feet in length, and, after the rough, outside bark was peeled off, was bent into the required shape. All around the top edge of the canoe, rim pieces, both inside and out, were fastened either with threads of bark or with splints. Across the bottom, inside, and up the sides were placed ribs at a distance apart of a few inches, which were fastened to the rims. Lengthwise, on the bottom was sometimes placed a thin, wide piece of wood on which to stand. Pitch was used in stopping seams and small holes. At the ends, which were pointed, the bark was united with the greatest care. One person usually paddled these canoes, while standing in the stern, except on long expeditions when several seated on alternate sides paddled the light canoe with great swiftness. By the use of this conveyance they passed quickly from point to point along their numerous lakes and rivers. The furs which the early traders bought of the Indians were brought a great distance in their easily contrived boats.

### SNOW SHOES

"The snow shoe is an Indian invention." [Morgan.] The white hunter quickly saw its utility and made it his inseparable companion on his long winter expeditions. With it he could travel farther on the snow than he could in summer on the ground. It was no unusual thing for a trapper to travel forty miles between sun and sun on a pair of snow shoes. At the same time he would carry a heavy load of traps or furs besides his gun and provisions. A piece of hickory or ash about one inch in diameter and six feet long was bent with the bow at the front end and brought to a point at the heel. Near the front it was from fourteen to eighteen inches across, and held in shape by cross pieces firmly fastened at each end to the rim or frame. Between these cross pieces and the outside frame, was a very strong netting of woven deer thongs, the meshes of which were about an inch across. At the fore part of this net work the ball of the foot was fastened, leaving the heel free, while the toes of the foot, at every step, naturally bent over the cross braids to

which the net work was fastened at the front.   If the
snow be slightly packed or frozen it will bear a man
who can easily run down heavy game.

### THE BABY FRAME

Another Indian invention was the baby frame.   It
was about two feet in length and twelve or fourteen
inches through, curved at the front, and having a bow
extending out over the front at the upper end.   The
mother exercised the greatest skill in ornamenting the
frame.   The baby was wrapped in a soft blanket and
placed in this frame, and a cover was thrown over the
arch or bow at the top.   When walking, the mother
fastened this frame to her back.   When working in
the field, she would hang it from some nearby support
and it would swing in the breeze.   Travellers tell us
that a baby would hang thus for hours and not make
a single complaint.

### BASKETS AND BOTTLES

The Indian women also showed much inventive genius in the baskets which they wove from splints, corn-
husks and flags.   The most perfectly finished of these
was the sieve basket, designed for sifting corn meal.
The bottom of the basket was woven so finely as to answer this purpose nearly as well as a wire sieve. [Mor-
gan.]   Another ingenious contrivance was the salt
bottle which was woven larger at the bottom than at
the top and looked not unlike a small wicker woven
demijohn.

### THE MOCCASIN

"The moccasin is preeminently an Indian invention,
and one of the highest antiquity." [Morgan.]   It was
made of a single piece of skin with a seam only at the
top and heel.   When not allowed to fall at the top, it
reached above the ankle where it was fastened with
deer strings.   There has never been made any outside
covering for the foot that was more nearly adapted to

the purpose for which it was designed. The needle was made from a bone found near the ankle joint of the deer. The thread was made from the sinews of the same animal. The deer skin is tanned by the use of the brains of the deer. These are dried in cakes for future use. The hair is scraped from the skin, after which the skin is soaked in a solution made by boiling the cake of brains in water. After a few hours it is wrung and stretched till it becomes pliable. Sometimes it is necessary to repeat this process. Afterward it is thoroughly smoked till the pores are full and the skin is tough It is then ready for use. The brains of some other animals were also used. Bear skins were not tanned but were left with the hair on for beds upon which to sleep. [Morgan.]

### INDIAN CORN

The Iroquois used three kinds of corn, White, Red and White Flint. When ripe they husked and braided it as our farmers do to-day and hung it in a dry place. It was their staple article of food, and they used it on nearly all occasions. They ground it in a mortar and sifted the meal in a sieve basket, and then baked it in loaves an inch thick and about six inches in diameter. This was the Indian bread. They also had a way of charring the corn which would cause it to keep for several years. Another way was to pick the corn when it was yet green and partially roast it, and then it was shelled and dried in the sun. With it was mixed about a third part of maple sugar and ground into flour. The hunter or warrior could subsist upon a small amount of this while on a long expedition. "This noble grain, one of the gifts of the Indian to the world, is destined, eventually, to become one of the staple articles of human consumption." [Morgan.]

# CHAPTER VI

## LEGENDS

Nearly all writers on Indian affairs tell us the Indian knew little if anything of the passion of love. , But the large number of love legends that have been handed down from generation to generation go to show that the dusky young people of the forest could love as truly as the more civilized white people.

In different parts of our State are to be found huge bluffs where the ledge of rock has either been raised nearly vertical by some great upheaval of the earth's crust, or has been worn away on one side so as to present an unbroken fall of from one to two hundred feet. These places are known as "Lovers' Leap." There is such a romantic spot near the city of Little Falls. The Indians have a very pretty legend connected with these places. Once upon a time, when one of the Iroquois nations was at war with the Algonquins, a brave and handsome young chief was taken prisoner and condemned to die. While awaiting the day of execution, he was fed by a beautiful Iroquois maiden, daughter of the chief. Her pity for the brave young warrior soon changed to love, and she determined to save his life. Watching her opportunity, one night when the sentinels, tired with their long vigil, had fallen asleep, she glided silently to his side and cut the cords which bound him, and whispered to him to follow her. Scarcely had they reached the river's brink when the shrill war whoop sounded on the night air, and they knew they were pursued. They had not gone a hundred rods before they saw a dozen hardy warriors in canoes rapidly gaining upon them. They paddled to the shore and climbed the rugged mountain on the brow of which they were discovered in the early morning light. The old chief, beside himself with anger, drew his bow to shoot the fugitive Algonquin, when the maiden stepped before him to shield him from her father. She plead for her lover's life, and said they would throw themselves from the precipice rather than be separated. Several warriors were sent forward to secure them, when the lovers, with a despairing cry, turned and threw themselves from the ledge and died together on the rocks below. Too late the stern father repented of his cruelty and wept over the tragic end of the life of his beautiful daughter.

### DISCOVERY OF MEDICINE

The Indians have some queer traditions concerning the discovery of medicinal plants. The following is one of these : ''An Indian hunter went forth to hunt, and as he wandered in the forest he heard a strain of beautiful music far off among the trees. He listened but could not tell whence it came, and knew it could not be by any human voice, or from any instrument he had ever heard. As he came near it ceased. The next evening he went forth again, but he heard not the music; and again, but in vain. Then came the Great Spirit to him in a dream and told him he must fast, and wash himself till he was purified, and then he might go forth, and he would hear again the music. So he purified himself and went again among the darkest trees of the forest. and soon his ear caught the sweet strains, and as he drew near they became more beautiful, and he listened till he had learned them and could make the same sweet sounds. .Then he saw that it was a plant with a tall green stem and long tapering leaves. He took his knife and cut the stalk, but ere he had scarcely finished, it healed and was the same as before. He cut it again, and again it healed, and then he knew it would heal diseases, and he took it home and dried it by the fire, and pulverized it, and applying a few particles of it to a dangerous wound, no sooner had it touched the flesh than it was whole. Thus the Great Spirit taught the Indian the nature of medicinal plants, and directed him where they were to be found.''

## THE PIGMIES AND GREAT BUFFALOES

The Pigmies were like folks, who lived in the far distant North where it was so cold that they could not grow to the stature of men and women. These little folks were always doing good to the family of man. The Great Buffaloes were huge monsters that lived on human flesh and travelled in great subterranean walks from which they would suddenly appear upon the earth and devour all the people in a village before they had time to escape. ''One day an Indian maiden was dipping water from a little brook, and as she bent over the stream, the water reflected a strange appearance. On looking up she beheld three Pigmies just alighting near where she stood. She knew immediately that there was danger, for they never at any other time made themselves visible to mortal eyes. The Pigmies knew where the Great Buffaloes had gone, and that they would soon return, and they bade the maiden flee to inform her people that they might be ready for flight if they should not succeed in their mission; but they told her they would meet her again at the stream and inform her if they were able to destroy them. When they had finished their message, with one stroke of their paddles the canoe arose in the air and sailed along over the tree tops a great distance, and then descended to the water, when another stroke bore it again aloft. When they reached the place where the buffaloes appeared, they cut down the largest hickory trees and split them in two parts for their bows, and made them arrows of the tallest pines of the forest. With these they pierced them and sent the arrows with such force that they passed through the monsters, who fell crushing whole forests beneath them. From their blood arose the small buffaloes, while their bones have remained undecayed for untold centuries.''

"The Pigmies, having accomplished their purpose, returned to inform the maiden at the stream, who listened to their story with delight, and ran to announce the glad tidings to her people, and then they departed to their northern home.''

### THE PLEIADES

The Pleiades, or Seven Stars, were placed in the heavens in the following manner :

"Seven little boys asked their mothers to permit them to make a feast; but they were denied. Still intent upon their purpose, they went alone and procured a little white dog to sacrifice, and while dancing around the fire, they were suddenly carried away through the air by some invisible spirit. Their mothers gazed after them with inconsolable anguish, till they saw them take their place in the sky among the starry hosts, where they are dancing still as the seven stars of the pleiades.''

### WITCHCRAFT

A belief in witchcraft seems to have been born in the American Indian From the very interesting writing of Schoolcraft I take the following, concerning this belief among the Iroquois :

"Among the Iroquois the belief was universal, and its effects upon their prosperity and population, if tradition is to be credited, were at times appalling. The theory of the popular belief, as it existed in the several cantons, was this : The witches and wizards constituted a secret association, which met at night to consult on mischief, and each was bound to inviolable secrecy.

They say this fraternity first arose among the Nanti-
cokes.   A witch or wizard had  power to turn into a
fox or wolf, and run very swift, emitting flashes of
light.    They could also transform themselves into a
turkey or big owl, and fly very fast.    If detected, or
hotly pursued, they could change into a stone or rotten
log.   They sought carefully to procure the poison of
snakes or poisonous roots, to effect their purposes.
They could blow hairs or worms into a person.''

The same authority recites a story told by Webster,
the naturalized Onondaga, who heard it from the lips
of an aged Onondaga.   This old man said that he had
formerly lived near the old church on the Kasoida
Creek, near Jamesville, where there was in old times  a
populous Indian village.   One evening, he said, whils't
he lived there he stepped out of his lodge, and immediately sank in the earth, and found himself in a large
room, surrounded by three hundred witches and wizards.    Next morning  he went to the council and told
the chiefs of this extraordinary occurrence.   They asked him whether he could not identify the persons.   He
said he could.   They then accompanied him on a  visit
to all the lodges, where he pointed out this and that
one, who were marked for execution.    Before this in-
quiry was ended, a  very large number of persons of
both sexes were killed.    Another tradition says that
about fifty persons were burned to death at the Onondaga castle for witches.

The delusion prevailed among all the cantons.    The
last persons executed for witchcraft among the Oneidas,
suffered about forty years ago.  They were two females.
The executioner was the notorious Hon Yost of revolu-
tionary memory.   He entered the lodge, according to a
prior decree of the Council, and struck them down with
a tomahawk.   One was found in the lodge; the other
suffered near the lodge door.

### ANCIENT WORSHIP

In Schoolcraft's notes on the Iroquois we read "that it was a striking peculiarity of the ancient religious system of the Iroquois that, once a year, the priesthood supplied the people with sacred fire. For this purpose, a set time was announced for the ruling priest's visit. The entire village was apprised of this visit, and the master of each lodge was expected to be prepared for this annual rite. Preliminary to the visit, his lodge fire was carefully put out and ashes scattered about it, as a symbolic sign of desolation and want. Deprived of this element, they were also deprived of its symbolic influence, the sustaining aid and countenance of the Supreme Power, whose image they recognized in the sun."

"It was to relieve this want, and excite hope and animation in breasts which had throbbed with dread, that the priest visited the lodge. Exhibiting the insignia of the sacerdotal office, he proceeded to invoke the Master of Life in their behalf, and ended his visit by striking fire from the flint, or from percussion, and lighting anew the domestic fire. The lodge was then swept and garnished anew, and a feast succeeded. This sacred service annually performed, had the effect to fix and increase the reverence of the people for the priestly office. It acted as a renewal of their ecclesiastical fealty; and the consequence was, that the institution of the priesthood was deeply and firmly seated."

### THE INDIAN YEAR

"Whether this rite had any connection with the period of the solstices, or with the commencement of the lunar year, is not known, but is highly probable. Their year was the lunar year. It consisted of thirteen moons, each of which is distinctly named. Thirteen moons of 28 days each, counting from visible phase to phase, make a year of 364 days, which is the greatest astronomical accuracy reached by the North American tribes."

# CHAPTER VII

## THE ONEIDA STONE

THE following excellent account of the historical
Oneida Stone was kindly furnished by the Rev. George
Hardy, of Sanquoit, N. Y.

Near the entrance of Forest Hill Cemetery, Utica, on
a slight artificial mound, is a roundish, oblong boulder
of gray syenite, known as the Oneida Stone. It was
an object of special veneration to the Indians of New
York, and especially to the Oneidas, the second of the
tribes of the Iroquois Confederacy. Indeed it gave
name to this tribe, and through them to many localities
in the State and elsewhere. The story of the Stone
contains much of legend mixed with certain facts of
veritable history. We will make no attempt to disen-
tangle these, but give the story as accepted by the Indians. In the Oneida speech, *onia* is stone; *oniota* is
child of the stone, or man of the stone. By mispro-
nunciation this became Oneida. The stone was heav-
en sent, a token of the presence of the Great Spirit. It
was given to the tribe at its very beginning, on the Oswego River, near Oneida Lake. To them it was sacred,
and became central in their religious and social life. It
was their alter of sacrifice. Around it were held the
feasts of New Year and harvest, and other festivals.
Beside it were their war dances and council fires. It
added solemn sanction to their treaties and other en-
gagements. Later, when the headquarters of the tribe
were removed to the eastern end of the lake near where
it receives the waters of Oneida Creek, the Stone accompanied them, untouched by human hands. The
same thing occurred at a subsequent removal up the

creek,—the stone taking position on a hill on the eastern side, in what is now the town of Stockbridge, in Madison Co.    Here it remained during the subsequent history of its people.    It here saw the rise and power of the confederacy of the Five Nations.    It here listened to wisdom and eloquence unsurpassed by Greek or Roman.    Logan, the white man's friend uttered words that burn.    Sconondoa, warrior-chief and last orator of his race, swayed the hearts of his fellow tribesmen. This was the resting place of the stone when the white man appeared in the land, and the red skinned children of the Great Spirit began to give way before him.    It saw the hunting grounds of its people becoming the corn fields of the stranger,    their forest-trails growing into his highways of traffic, their hills and valleys filled and crowned with his settlements.    It saw its people themselves waste away at the stranger's presence,    their council fires extinguished, their festal days unobserved, their sacrifices unoffered.    It saw them diminished and scattered, their tribal life lost, and their political power forever gone.    "It was a stranger in the home of its children, an exile on its own soil."    Awhile after the opening of the Forest Hill Cemetery, the Oneida Stone was, by glad consent of all parties interested, removed to its present location, there to be cared for as a memorial of a people who showed many excellences of character, and took no insignificant part in some of the exciting incidents of our nation's history.

# CHAPTER VIII

## GAMES

WE are largely indebted to that excellent work, Morgan's League of the Iroquois, for a description of the six principal games of the Six Nations. These were played both at their religious festivals, and on special days set apart for celebration. Challenges were sent from village to village, or from tribe to tribe, and not infrequently from the stranger tribes or nations. When these formal challenges were lacking, frequently a village separated into two divisions, not unlike our old fashioned spelling schools, each division striving for the mastery.

### GAMBLING

Betting was common among the Indians, and it was not unusual for one of them to gamble away all the property which he might possess; "his tomahawk, his medal, his ornaments and even his blankets."

### THE BALL GAME

Of all the games played by these people, the ball game was the one most favored. The bat used was about five feet long and looked not unlike a tennis racket split lengthwise. The ball was made of deer skin. There were six or eight players on each side. The field was about eighty rods across, with a gate on each side, which was simply two upright poles about three rods apart. One of these gates belonged to each party and the contest was to see which party would first carry the ball through its own gate a given number of times. In preparing for games of strength, skill and endurance, the contestant often went through a rigid course of dieting and training. He entered the lists naked except that he wore a waist cloth. The players were stationed in parallel lines, each side opposite of its own gate. The ball was dropped between the two rows where were stationed one player from each side. These two immediately began a contest for the possession of the ball. Great skill and dexterity was displayed until one or the other would succeed in sending it into the field among his own party. Then began a lively skirmish between the two parties to see which side could first force the ball through its own gate. The game often lasted the entire afternoon, and not infrequently was finished on the succeeding day. If one of the players was injured, he left the field and his place was filled with another from his party. The Indian was peculiarly fitted for this game.

### THE GAME OF JAVELINS

The game of javelins did not require the skill nor the endurance that was needed in playing ball. In this there was required a ring about eighteen inches in diameter, and each player had from three to six javelins. The contending parties were drawn up in two separate lines facing each other. One party rolled the ring in front of the other party who threw their javelines at it. If one of the party struck the ring, it was set up for a target at the spot where it was hit, and each man was required to throw his javelin at it. Those javelins, which hit the target thus thrown, were saved; those which passed the target without hitting it became the property of the other side and were thrown at the ring by them. Those javelins which hit were thus won and laid out of the play, while those which missed went to the rightful owners. Then the ring was rolled by the other party, and the foregoing was repeated. This was continued until one side had lost all their javelins, which decided the contest.

### THE GAME OF DEER BUTTONS

The game of deer buttons was a fireside game and was played with eight buttons about an inch in diameter made of elk horn, and were blackened upon one side. The players seated themselves upon a blanket spread out for the purpose. Near them was a certain number of beans piled upon the floor. One of the players would take the eight buttons in his hand, shake them, and throw them on the blanket. If all turned up the same color, the player took twenty beans from the pile, if six turned up of the same color, he took two beans; if seven, he took four. He continued to throw so long as not less than six of the same color turned up, when the throw passed to the other player. Thus they continued till the beans were in the possession of the two players, after which the loser was obliged to pay forfeit from his own stock till one man won them all. Any number could play this game at the same time, but each one had to give up two, four or twenty beans for each lucky throw of the opposing side.

### THE GAME OF SNOWSNAKES

The game of snowsnakes was played only in the winter season. The snakes were carefully made of the toughest hickory and were about one fourth of an inch thick and in width tapered from one inch at the head to half an inch at the foot, and were six or seven feet in length. The head was round and turned up like a sleigh runner, and was tipped with lead. These were played by skillfully throwing them so that they would run or slide a great distance over the frozen snow. The number of players was limited and selected with the greatest care. After the place had been selected and the direction determined, the snakes were thrown by the contending parties. That snake which ran the greatest distance was a point for the side to which it

belonged. These contests were repeated till one side
had won the necessary number of points.

### THE BOW AND ARROW

"In archery the Indian has scarcely been excelled.
With a quick eye and a powerful muscle, he could send
his arrow as unerringly as the archers of Robin Hood."
To be the best marksman in the tribe was considered
a great honor. The bow was three or four feet in
length and very strong, so that when the string was
well drawn back it sent an arrow with great swiftness.
It required the greatest muscular strength to use such
a weapon. The arrow was about three feet long,
pointed with flint or other hard substance, and at its
small end were fastened feathers in a spiral form which
caused it to revolve. This gave it a horizontal direction and may have been what suggested the grooved
rifle barrel. Morgan tells us that the Scottish and
English archers tipped their arrows with straight
feathers.

### LEAPING AND WRESTLING

He further says that leaping, wrestling and other
gymnastic exercises appeared to be no part of their
public amusement. Very often in hand to hand contests the white man exhibited more skill in boxing
and could throw his Indian opponent, but could not
keep him down when thrown.

### THE FOOT RACE

There was one exercise in which the Indian greatly
excelled, viz: the foot race. Situated as the six nations were they needed runners to carry messages
from nation to nation and it was a matter of national
pride to have the swiftest runner. There grew up a
spirit of emmulation which resulted in regular contests.
The competitors often went through a course of training and dieting as the more civilized athlete does to-day.

### THE PEACH STONE GAME

From ancient times it was customary to close the Green Corn and Harvest festivals and the New Year's jubilee with the Peach Stone game. So much did they admire this game that they believed they would enjoy it in the future life in the realm of the Great Spirit. Six peach stones, which had been ground down so that the pit could be removed, were blackened upon one side. These were thrwon into a wooden or earthern dish and the count depended upon the number of one kind that came up similar to the game of deer buttons already explained except that nothing less than five of a kind counted instead of six. It often took the greater part of two days to play this game, and simple as it may seem, it usually produced great excitement throughout the tribes whose representatives were engaged. I quote again from Morgan. "Among the Iroquois, in the celebration of their national games, as far as they went, is to be found the same species of enthusiasm and emulation which characterized the celebration of the games of antiquity. Although the national games, like the popular songs of one people, may be incapable of exciting the enthusiasm or awakening the patriotic spirit of another; yet they are not, for this reason, devoid of interest. If it be asked what interest for us can attach to these games of the Iroquois, one answer at least may be given:—they show that the American wilderness, which we have been taught to pronounce a savage solitude until the white men entered its borders, had long been vocal in its deepest seclusions, with the gladness of human hearts."

# CHAPTER IX

## EARLY EXPLORERS

WHEN Cartier ascended the St. Lawrence he found a large village occupying the present site of Montreal surrounded with crops of waving corn. It was occupied by a tribe of Indians which the French named the Iroquois. They treated the white men with great reverence, as if they were divine, even bringing their sick and laying them before the French that their presence might heal them. Cartier, returning to Quebec, betrayed the confidence of the natives by forcing their head chief and several of his followers on board and taking them to France where they died. Four years later he returned and attempted to plant a colony. But the Indians, remembering Cartier's former conduct, lost faith in the white man and his black robed priests, and consequently did not show their former kindness. The French leader became discouraged and set sail for France. About the same time Roberval attempted to establish a colony on the same site, but being unfitted by nature for a leader of men his attempt resulted in failure and for nearly seventy years the St. Lawrence furnished music for none but savage ears. [Doyle's English Colonies in America.]

## CHAMPLAIN

The French were the first Europeans to intrude upon the domain of the Iroquois. It was given to Samuel DeChamplain to carry his faith and his nationality into the heart of the territory of the amphictyonic league, and by so doing he forever ruined all prospects of winning the haughty Iroquois and his land for the French crown. He was a French soldier anxious to build a great empire in the New World. Nearly seventy years after Roberval left Quebec, Champlain and DeMonts re-established a colony at that place. They gained the good will of the surrounding red men, and the war trained Frenchman, Champlain, could not resist the entreaties of the Hurons to aid them in their expeditions against their powerful enemies, the Iroquois. They ascended the outlet of Lake Champlain on the west bank of which they encountered a large force of the Iroquois. [Colden.] Champlain placed himself at the head and shot down three of the enemy, who were astonished beyond measure at the sound of the white man's gun. The Hurons seeing the disorder in the ranks of the enemy rushed forward and gained a signal victory. The place of this battle was at or near Ticonderoga in Essex county, a place destined to be the scene of many a skirmish in after years. Such was the Iroquois' introduction to the Frenchmen, one which they never forgot and never wholly forgave. The echoes of Champlain's guns did not cease to reverberate till they died away on the Plains of Abraham. Had he come among them as did Penn among the Delawares several years later, French History on American soil would have been much different from what it was. The year following Champlain gained another victory over them on the river Sorel. In the Autumn of this same year still anxious to press his conquests south of the St. Lawrence he again lead the Hurons against their ancient enemies. He crossed the outlet of Lake Ontario and coasted along its eastern shore for many miles. At some point within the present limits of Jefferson county they hid their canoes and marched overland to Oneida Lake. South of this, perhaps in Madison county, they found a fort, strongly palisaded surrounded by ditches so that they could neither take the place by storm nor set it on fire. Champlain was wounded and was compelled to retreat from the country followed for many miles by the infuriated barbarians. This ended Champlain's work in the present limits of New York south of the great river; and by his policy the Anglo Saxons aided by the powerful Six Nations eventually became the dominant race.

## THE DUTCH AND THE IROQUOIS

In the fall of 1609 Henry Hudson sailed up the great North River. About five years later the Dutch established a trading post just south of the present site of Albany. Thither flocked the Indians with furs to exchange for articles which the white man had to sell. At the same time the French were trying to secure the trade with the tribes in this part of the country and came up Lake Champlain in boats for that purpose. Thus early in the seventeenth century the French and the Dutch became commercial rivals in the New World. After a short time this trading post was abandoned and in 1617 a fort was erected at the mouth of the Tawasentha. The Dutchmen with an eye to business formed a treaty with the surrounding Indian tribes, perhaps the first ever made with the red men. The Iroquois were leaders in bringing about this treaty of peace while the other tribes were considered as their subjects. They buried the tomahawk and the white men promised to erect a church over the place as a sign of perpetual peace. These traders builded with the Indians better than they knew. The treaty of Tawasentha lasted as long as the Dutch held possession of the country, and did much to hold the friendship of the great barbaric league. The contrast between the treatment accorded the Iroquois by Champlain and the treatment by the Dutch was so great. that the latter had the confidence of these tribes and could depend upon their alliance. They respected the rights of the Indians, paid for the lands which they occupied and in their dealings were influenced by rules of justice and equity. They were not zealots, neither did they come to conquer the country and form a great empire in the New World. They were largely traders and encouraged peace with their savage neighbors as the surest road to money getting.

Early in the history of Fort Orange an incident occured which might nave created hard feeling on the part of the Mohawks. A party of Mohicans on their way to attack their ancient enemies, the Mohawks, induced a few Dutchmen to join them. The Mohawks gained a signal victory and the Dutch leader and three of his men lost their lives. The Mohawks claimed to have acted on the defensive, so the Dutch wisely let the matter drop. Shortly after this the Mohicans were driven from their beautiful hunting grounds on the Hudson by their ancient enemies. All the river Indians were subject to the Mohawks and in the winter of 1643 a large party of them marched down the west bank of the Hudson to collect tribute from the tribes living there. These fled in terror and sought refuge with the Dutch in and around Manhattan. Had Kieft pursued a course dictated by reason and humanity he would have befriended them and won their lasting regard. But he gave orders to have them cruelly massacred. This aroused all the surrounding tribes who started upon the war path destroying whole villages spreading terror and destruction wherever they went. This state of things continued nearly two years when the governor made treaties with several of the tribes even going with much pomp to the land of the Mohawks. They made a preliminary treaty with him at Fort Orange afterward confirmed by a large gathering of Indians at Fort Amsterdam, at which time a party of Mohawks came as arbitrators for the Five Nations. Stuyvesant as Governor renewed friendly alliances with the powerful Mohawks. Indeed so often did this nation act as arbitrators between the Dutch and River Indians that great jealousy was aroused on the part of the latter. In 1661 Arendt van Curler was sent to purchase the "Great Flats" where Schenectady now stands. Nearly twenty years before he had penetrated far into the country of the Mohawks. In all of the years that he had dealings with the western Indians he treated them with the greatest kindness, and to him more than to any other man was due the peaceful settlement of the Mohawk Valley. In 1667 he was drowned in Lake Champlain, the crystal clearness of whose waters is a type of his dealings with the unfortunate red men.

# CHAPTER X

AFTER the destruction of the Pequots on the Mystic river, Sassacus, knowing that the English would soon attack his tribe, determined to march westward and throw himself on the mercies of the Mohawks. He did not seem to understand the fierceness of this tribe, for as soon as they saw him they cruelly shot him. The handful of his followers who escaped the English were finally assigned lands by the Mohawks near Lake Champlain.

## THE ERIES

About 1643, according to Schoolcraft, the Senecas aided by some of the other members of the confederacy, began a war with the Eries and their allies, the andastes. These Indians lived near Lake Erie and were known to the French as the Neuter Indians. They were given this name because they kept aloof from all the wars of the surrounding tribes. Cusic, the Indian historian, says "That delegates from a northern nation, with whom the Iroquois were at war, having been received by the Eries, Yagowanea, the female ruler of the tribe, at Kienuka, on the Niagara Ridge betrayed the Seneca deputation to their concealed enemies from the North, by whom they were killed." This was in violation of their neutrality and the Iroquois flew to arms. The war was short and bloody. There could be but one outcome. The Six Nations so long accustomed to wage war successfully with large and powerful tribes soon conquered the Eries, and as a nation they disappeared from history. Mr. Evans who wrote in 1755 says those who survived fled to the valley of the Ohio and later still crossed the Alleghanies.

### THE HURONS

After the Hurons had united with the French, the Iroquois became their most bitter enemies. The whole country from the Oswego, Genessee and Niagara rivers, even to Montreal, was covered with war parties. Both of the same race, they carried on the fight with the bitterness of a family quarrel. A journey of a thousand miles was cheerfully undertaken by an Iroquois if only he could glut his savage revenge. The Andastes, who could have sent a band of nearly 1.500 warriors, offered to assist the Hurons. They refused assistance and alone attempted to defend themselves and their country; but by 1647 the Huron tribe was brought to great straights and were compelled to seek shelter under the guns of Quebec. Even here they were not safe and were finally driven from the valley of the St Lawrence about the year 1659. They fled up the great Ottowas river and across to the Manitoulin chain of islands. But the merciless Iroquois would give them no peace and they sought refuge on the shores of Lake Superior. Here again they were attacked by their relentless enemies and a great many of them cruelly massacred. This place is still known as Point Iroquois.

### THE ANDASTES

In 1661 the Senecas began to carry on a desultory warfare with the Andastes. The latter gained a few small victories when the Senecas raised an army of 1,600 warriors and marched into their country and beseiged a small fort. The Andastes held out bravely and at last, sallying out, they drove the Senecas in headlong flight. This victory earned them not a small amount of fame, and caused some of them, harassed by their incursions, to move north of Lake Ontario. But from this time their power began to wane. Prisoners were taken sometimes by one Iroquois tribe and sometimes by another.  Schoolcraft relates that a party of 60 Andastes boys engaged a party of Senecas and put them to flight.  But by the year 1675 they had been subdued by the Iroquois.

# CHAPTER XI

It was about this time, 1664, that the English compelled the Dutch to surrender their rights to the present limits of New York. The relations between the Dutch and Iroquois were very friendly. The sturdy Hollander had almost the entire trade with the Five Nations, and had extended his influence even beyond the Great Lakes. Even long after the advent of the English, he acted as interpreter. When the Iroquois learned that the English had taken the place of the Dutch, they at once admitted them into their confidence, and the English, on their part, did their utmost to preserve the friendship of this powerful confederacy. Their enemies became the enemies of the Iroquois and their friends, the friends of the latter. The English soon learned that the French wished to acquire the beautiful Mohawk valley and if possible extend their conquest to the ocean itself. The Six Nations were a tower of strength for the English against the encroachments of the French. Schoolcraft says "who can read the details of an hundred years' sanguinary contests, without perceiving that it was the undying vigilance, the unerring accuracy of their geographical knowledge of the wilderness, and the manly bravery of the Iroquois, which, up to the year 1775, preserved western New York to the English crown?''

Champlain had furnished neighboring tribes with guns, powder and knives which they used in their wars against the Iroquois. When the Dutch came they could secure these coveted weapons and soon became a terror not only to the surrounding tribes, but

to the French themselves. They successfully repelled
the invasions of La Barre, Denonville and Frontenac,
and for a long time resisted the establishment of French
missions at Oneida, Onondaga and Ontario. The introduction of fire arms entirely changed the Indian
mode of fighting. They took longer and more frequent excursions, and no tribe was able to withstand
them; while the council fire at Onondaga burned
brighter than ever before. The English early established an agency among the Mohawks which, by a
slow growth, in time fully protected English interests.

### FRENCH IN THE MOHAWK VALLEY

In 1665 Concelles, governor of Canada, sent a party
against the Mohawks. They travelled on snow shoes
suffering greatly from the cold. They got as far as
Schenectady where the Indians would have defeated
them had it not been for the hospitality of Corlear who
had great influence with the Mohawks. The next
spring, twelve light companies of foot, and the whole
militia of Canada marched into the country of the Mohawks, who retired into the forests on the approach of
the enemy. Although the French were unable to subdue the Mohawks, yet through a great parade of
strength and the Indian's fear of fire arms, a peace
was concluded in 1667 which lasted several years. The
French governor improved this cessation of hostilities
by sending out missionaries, building forts and estab-
lishing trading posts. In 1672 he penetrated as far as
Oneida Lake where he started to build a fort, which
Count Frontenac completed the following year.

### SIR WILLIAM JOHNSON

Sir William Johnson, on being appointed superintendent of Indian affairs, assembled a very large number of Indians at his place on the Mohawk and announced his appointment to the.n. He made offers to
them to restore their confidence in the English and to

counteract French influence. He eloquently plead with them to send their warriors on Braddock's expedition. They promptly told him that the governor of Virginia had occupied their lands in the Ohio valley and so they would not assist him. However they agreed to remain neutral. They also declined to accompany Shirley in his expedition to Oswego. But they promptly sent a large body of warriors to meet Deiskau at Crown Point where they fought with great bravery losing their leader, King Hendrick.

Johnson's victory, which was really earned by Lyman, at Crown Point, was the turning point in the ascendency of the British influence with the Iroquois and their allies, which had been at a very low ebb at the commencement of the French war. The unearned fame which Johnson acquired raised him greatly in the estimation of the Iroquois. The triumph at Lake George, in which King Hendrick lost his life, presaged events soon to transpire. England, advised by such men as Johnson, clearly saw that whoever conquered would control the Indians, and she prepared for a great struggle. In a very general council, convened at his hall, April 19, 1767, Johnson made a long speech to the representatives not only of the Iroquois but many other Indians. He attempted to prove to them that the French were deceiving the Indians and would not keep their promises, but that if they held with the English, their lands and their lodges would be protected. Said he, "Tell them, from me, to look at the French forts, built and building through the middle of their country, and on their best building lands. Let them look at French flags, flying in their forts at all the great lakes, along the great rivers, in order to oblige them to trade with the French only, and sell their skins, and take goods from them at what prices the French may please to put on them. And it is a thing well known to all Indians, that the French cannot sell their goods near as cheap as the English can.''

## CROWN POINT

The expedition against Crown Point was in charge of General Wm. Johnson with Colonel Lyman second in command. The latter made all the military plans for Johnson, and preceded him in the hot summer days to a place about fifty miles from Albany, the great "carrying place" between Lake Champlain and Albany. Here he constructed a fort and named it "Fort Lyman." Later in the season Johnson, who, according to Lossing, had neither the courage nor the skill of a good general, arrived at the place on his way to Crown Point. Discouraged by Braddock's defeat and knowing that the French were gaining a kindly interest on the part of the Iroquois, he would have given up the expedition had it not been for Lyman. He finally constructed a camp on Lake George without entering it or making proper fortifications. Hearing that the woods to the north were filled with French and Indians, he sent Colonel Williams with a detachment of provincials accompanied by King Hendrick with a band of Mohawk warriors. They all fell into an ambuscade and Williams and Hendrick and many of their followers were killed. Those who escaped from the carnage fled to Johnson's headquarters. He succeeded in felling a breastwork of trees and bringing into action two large guns which did much to check the rush of the motley crowd of French and Indians.

Just at this point Lyman marched upon the scene with his small army and took charge of the battle, Johnson having retired with a slight flesh wound. The battle raged furiously for several hours when the French commander received a mortal wound and his followers fled leaving Lyman a victor. Had Johnson taken advantage of the panic in the French army he

could have captured Crown Point and perhaps have
driven the enemy into Canada. We have described
this action at some length because of the prominent
part taken by the Mohawks and the great loss which
they sustained in the death of their leader, Soiengar-
ahta, popularly known as "King Hendrick." Schoolcraft tells that he was a chief of high standing among
the Mohawks, of approved wisdom, undoubted tre-
pidity, and a firm friend of the English. He had visited
England, and had been presented at court. He united
great amenity of manners, dignity of bearing, and
mild features, to the most determined courage and energy. The band of warriors which he led are said to
have "fought like lions." In comparing his judgment as a general with that of Johnson's, it is said that
when the latter wished to send a small company to
meet the French, Hendrick said, "If they are to fight
they are too few; if they are to be killed they are too
many." He easily stood in the first rank of the Indian statesmen of his age. The following story has
been handed down from his time.

Once when visiting at Johnson Hall he saw an em-
broidered scarlet coat, such a one as was frequently
worn by English officers of that day. He became possessed of a strong desire to own it, which desire he
satisfied in the following manner : One morning he
said to Johnson, "Brother, me dream last night."
"Indeed," said Johnson, "What did my red brother
dream?" "Me dream that coat be mine." Johnson,
thoroughly understanding Indian nature, promptly
said, "Brother, the coat is yours." Some time after
this, the Indian commissioner made a visit to King
Hendrick, and one morning said to him, "My red
brother, I dreamed last night." "What did my white
brother dream?" Hendrick asked. "I dreamed," replied the wily Johnson, "that you gave me this tract

of land," and he described a section of land with certain natural boundaries, including about 100,000 acres. Hendrick was astonished, hesitated a few moments, and replied, "The land is yours, but do not dream again." England confirmed the title, and it was known for many years as "The Royal Grant." The writer can remember when the older residents called the present village of Deveraux, in Fulton County, the "Corner of the Grant."

# CHAPTER XII

Courage has been admired by all men from the remotest period, and he is the bravest man who resolutely faces a known danger. No braver set of men ever lived than those who penetrated the savage wilderness to establish Christian Missions for the conversion of the Indians. Many of them were cruelly tortured and put to death in the most revolting and shocking manner. Yet their zeal never waned. They were actuated by a desire to spread Christianity; all French missionaries were anxious to extend French influence and to form a great French empire in the New World. Somewhere about the year 1640 or 1641, the Iroquois conceived the idea of making a sort of treaty with the French, but did not wish to have their Indian allies included in the treaty. These terms were promptly rejected by the French. The Iroquois quickly prepared for war. A large party of them captured, on the St. Lawrence, three Frenchmen accompanying several boat loads of Hurons to the Huron Country. Many of the Christian Indians were killed and a few taken prisoners. One of the captives was an Indian maiden who, tradition says, married a Mohawk chief and was long remembered for her virtues and intelligence. She exerted a marked influence among the Mohawks, and many interesting stories are told concerning her goodness. The three Frenchmen were led from town to town along the Mohawk river for a week or more. Their finger nails were torn off, and pieces of flesh were cut from their backs. They were made to run the gauntlet, and then they were tied to stakes while the children and youths amused themselves by throwing live coals upon them. At last one of them was killed, and a second who had shown great bravery was adopted iuto the tribe. The third Frenchman, who was no other than Isaac Jogues, the accomplished scholar and zealous priest, was retained by them and became a missionary to these barbarians. The customs of the Mohawks were revolting to a man of such a refined nature. He saw captives burned at the stake and their flesh eaten. Van Curler. who was at this time a Dutch Commissary, hearing of the treatment that Jogues was receiving, made a journey into the country of the Mohawks. The Indians received him kindly, but would not accept his offers for the release of the missionary. Later, on an expedition to Fort Orange, he made his escape and was befriended by the great Dutch preacher, Rev. Megapolensis. Money was donated so that he was able to return to his native country where he was received with signal marks of honor.

After some time he returned to this country and acted in the capacity of peace agent between the Canadian French and the Iroquois. His knowledge of the Indian character made him fairly successful on this journey. Some time after this he returned to found a mission among the Iroquois, but in some manner while he had been away from the Indians, they had acquired a superstitious fear of him, and as soon as he made his appearance among them, he and his companions were cruelly tortured and put to death.

# CHAPTER XIII

## THE REVOLUTION

When we consider that the colonies were surrounded by hostile tribes of Indians numbering many thousands of souls, nearly all under the influence of the British who had been fifteen years winning the affections of the tribes from the French; the cruelty of savage warfare; the great resources of the mother country on land and sea; we are astonished at the courage of our forefathers in attempting to cut loose from England. To cope with the ablest generals that a powerful nation could send, required a skill in war unheard of on the part of young and undeveloped colonies. But at the same time to cope with an unknown number of barbarians instigated and often led by still more savage white men was an undertaking frought with the greatest danger. The colonists went into the struggle with the warwhoop ringing in their ears, and visions of midnight massacres before their eyes. Schoolcraft estimates that the English employed 770 warriors in this sanquinary struggle, whose tomahawks and scalping knives were employed on the frontiers of New York, Pennsylvania and Virginia. It has been fully established that a bounty had been placed upon the scalps of the settlers, to incite the savage desires of an ever vengeful foe. It was only through war that the Indian character could develop and the Indian could win renown. He longed for war as the highway to glory. On the one hand British emissaries represented that the war was commenced by the colonists, a case of son against father, and that there could be but one outcome—for how could a few colonists cope with so powerful a nation?

On the other hand the Americans represented that the Six
Nations had no part in the quarrel and should remain
neutral, and then it would matter not which party
might win, their lands would be safe.  But the Indian's
horizon, bounded only by his tribal relations, could not
understand the rights and justice of nations.  He loved
war, and treacherous by nature, he preferred always to
be on the winning side.  He feared also that if the
Americans should win he would lose his hunting
grounds by the onward movement of the settlers.  Already the fur bearing animals were growing scarce or
disappearing altogether.  Great sections of their land,
the home of their forefathers, had been bargained away
by their chiefs for a few paltry trinkets.  It was natural that the Indian would seek vengeance on those whom
he found occupying these lands.  And it seemed the
weaker and more helpless the victim, the greater the
cruelty displayed by Indian nature.  In the face of all
these difficulties how could the colonists hope to win
over the Six Nations to neutrality?  And yet their efforts met with partial success.  In Schoolcraft's History of the Indian Tribes we read that "The Mohicans,
of Stockbridge, ranged themselves on the side of the
Americans, and performed good service as scouts
throughout the contest.  The Oneidas did the same.
The voice of the popular chief, Skenandoah, was heard
in favor of the rising colonies; and the watchful and
quick eye of Attatea, known as Colonel Louis, carefully
noted the approach of evil footsteps during the great
struggle of 1777, and gave every day the most reliable
information of the march and position of the enemy."
To the foregoing might be added at least a part of the
Tuscaroras, who were influenced by the Rev. Kirkland,
a resident for many years among the Oneidas, and one
small clan of the Mohawks at the lower castle.  All
the rest of the Six Nations aided the English.  Their

military skill and their knowledge of the country allied
with great native cunning and treachery made them the
most dreaded foe with which the Americans ever con-
tended. Circumstances brought the Iroquois under
that very capable guerilla leader, Thyendanagea, better
known as Joseph Brant, who had been brought up under the direction of Sir Wm. Johnson. Schoolcraft
says "he hated the Americans as Attila did the Romans."

Sir Wm. Johnson died suddenly in 1774 at just the
time he was so much needed by the English in shap-
ing the Indian policy to the advantage of the mother
country. "He disappeared from the scene of action
at a critical period, when, to employ an Indian alle-
gory, two thunder clouds, black with anger, seemed
rushing into conflict, leaving no one of sufficient capacity to cope with or control the storm. Great
Britain had lavished on him the highest honors, and
he was held in the highest respect by the Indians."
Continuing, Schoolcraft says, "Those who have inves-
tigated the proceedings and the character of Sir John
Johnson, of Guy Johnson his deputy, of Colonel Claus,
and of the various subordinates, who thenceforth controlled the direction of Indian affairs, have arrived at
the conclusion, that this important interest was man-
aged in a bad way, if their object was to serve the
Crown. The encouragement of murders and massacres
was well calculated to arouse the deepest hostility of
the colonists, and to cement them in the closest bonds
of unity against the oppression of the British yoke.
Numbers of persons, previously lukewarm in their
cause, were driven to take an active part in the contest by deeds of blood and Indian atrocity. The several conferences, held in the office of the British De-
partment, during the years '75 and '76, proved the in-
capacity of Sir William's successors to control great

events.   The Six Nations were, as a body, the friends
of the British, and did not like to see their officials, in
public councils, and by  public letters to committees
and corporations, palliating or denying acts which they
had secretly approved, and had  stimulated them to
perform.''   The patriots had no  faith in the kindly
intentions of Guy Johnson, and Washington  wrote  a
letter to Schuyler saying  ''watch the movements of
the Indian Agent, Colonel Guy Johnson, and prevent,
so far as you can, the effect  of his  influence, to  our
prejudice, with the  Indians.''  Johnson  well knew
that his every movement was  watched  and  he  heard
frequent  rumors that a body of patriots was coming to
arrest him.   He sent a letter  to  the  Oneidas  stating
this and asking them for the sake of old friendship  to
come to  his aid.   This letter was intercepted and fell
into patriot hands.   The Rev. Kirkland was urged  to
use  his influence to turn the friendship of the Oneidas
from the English to  the  colonists.   Brant,  who  was
Johnson's secretary, had  a dissolute sachem prefer
charges against Mr. Kirkland to Johnson with the object of getting the missionary removed.   The Oneidas
rallied to the support of their  pastor and  Brant  was
baffled for the time being, although later, as it appears
from Mr. Kirkland's letters, Johnson ordered him  not
only to remain away from the Oneidas, but not even to
speak to them.   Johnson arrested travelers on their way
up the Mohawk and searched them to see that they did
not carry messages to the Indians.   All this  time  he
was  in active  correspondence with the committees of
Tryon county, and to other  patriots claiming  that
he was unjustly persecuted.

In May a council of the Mohawk Chiefs was held at
Guy Park, a  beautiful spot on  the  Mohawk river.
This was attended  by the committees of Albany and
Tryon counties.   Little Abraham, who seems to  have

been the leading Mohawk Chief at this time, was the principal speaker. Among other things he said that ·'the Indians did not wish to have a quarrel with the white people, nor did they wish to have their supply of powder cut off. If it is we shall distrust you, we are willing to communicate with you in the presence of our Superintendent." It was evident from his speech that they were wholly under the influence of Johnson. As the Western Indians, who had been invited, were not present at this council, the Superintendent called another to take place farther west at Crosby's Manor. In June of this year a letter was addressed to Johnson asking him to use his influence to keep the Indians from committing depredations, and to hold themselves neutral from a contest that in no wise concerned them. This letter pointed out to him the risk he ran, as owner of a great estate in that locality, of calling upon himself the enmity of his neighbors. Johnson's reply to this letter threw the blame of the existing state of affairs on the colonists. He showed why he had been compelled to fortify his residence and he denied having stopped travelers on their journey except in the case of two New Englanders. He did not hold the council at Crosby's Manor, but moved his retinue to Fort Stanwix. This caused no small speculation and concern on the part of the patriot settlers of the Mohawk Valley. After a short respite he moved still farther West to Ontario where he held a conference with the Indians uninterrupted by the whites. He was much annoyed that supplies and messages were constantly intercepted while being conveyed to him. It was from this place that he wrote a letter to Mr. Livingston burning with loyalty, and filled with complaints of Herkimer and other patriots who had interfered with his affairs in the Mohawk Valley. He also stated that his conference with the

Indians was perfectly satisfactory to himself, he having convened 1340 warriors. There was also present at this council his Secretary, Brant, and the noted Butler and his son Walter. There was present of the Six Nations at least the Senecas, Cayugas and some of the Mohawks who had not emigrated to Canada. When we consider the close alliance that had existed between the Iroquois and the British for more than 100 years, we wonder that Johnson did not have more influence with the Oneidas and Tuscaroras. This council served to alarm the whole of the Mohawk Valley, and Herkimer wrote that he had positive information that Johnson would soon move down the river, and beginning just below Little Falls, would devastate the entire region eastward. The fact that Sir John had remained at Johnson Hall backed by a large following of loyalists lent color to this report. Some preparations for defence were made, but it was soon learned that Johnson had gone to Oswego where he drew up a treaty with the Indians. A little later, accompanied by several Iroquois chiefs, he journeyed to Montreal, evidently for the purpose of getting the influence of Sir Guy Carleton to firmly cement the friendship of the Indians to the Crown. It was at the conference at Oswego, according to Lossing, that Johnson invited the Six Nations to "feast on a Bostonian and drink his blood." Stone also mentions this in his Life of Brant. Although it was a figurative speech, it was taken up by the patriots as a sort of battle cry to arouse the passons of their more lukewarm neighbors.

To attempt to counteract the influence of the Johnsons' and if possible to keep the Six Nations neutral in the impending struggle a commission of five men was appointed to treat with the Indians. General Philip Schuyler was a member of this committee. An assembly was soon called at Albany where many speeches were made both by members of the committees and by the leading orators among the Indians. One of these was Little Abraham. In the main his speech was pacific. He however complained that the colonists had taken two large sections of land from the Mohawks for which they had not payed "so much as a pipe." He demanded that these be restored, for "if they are not and you win in this contest, you will take us by the arm and pull us all off." A pretty true prophecy of what did occur in after years. Little Abraham claimed that at the Oswego Council Johnson advised the Indians to remain neutral. This was a great surprise to the commissioners as it did not well accord with Johnson's actions, nor with the silent preparations which Sir John was making at the old residence on the Mohawk. He was surrounded by a sort of body guard of Scotch retainers who had settled on his lands in and about Johnstown. In Campbell's Annals we read that committees were appointed to "keep an eye on Sir John and his doings." It was one of these that deposed Sheriff White and lodged him in jail at Albany.

The Whigs declared that Sir John was in communication with Guy Johnson in Canada, and that powder was furnished the Indians from that source. Finally it was determined to ascertain just where Sir John stood in the war, and a committee was sent to ask whether they might have the free use of the Court House and whether he would permit the Scotch settlers to form into companies in the patriot service. Sir John replied that he never prevented their use of the court house nor the Scotch from enlisting in the patriot service. But as for himself "he would not lift his hand against the King even to prevent his head from being cut off."

When it was learned from one Connell that a large

amount of ammunition had lately been received at Johnstown, Congress ordered General Schuyler to proceed at once to that place and disarm and intimidate the Loyalists. It was thought proper to inform the Mohawks of the Lower Castle, who according to Stone, had not been drawn away by Brant, of this order. The Mohawks were displeased and showed great love and anxiety for Sir John. General Schuyler did not wait for the return of the messenger but marched at once towards Johnstown. At Schenectady he met Little Abraham who made a long speech, the under current of which showed much dissatisfaction that the patriot army was marching into the country of the Six Nations, and he urged upon Schuyler to be careful what he was doing. The General made a long speech to them which seemed satisfactory. He told them that their representatives might be present at the interview with Sir John.

There were constant additions to his forces during the next day till he had about 3000 followers. Before reaching Johnstown he was met by Sir John who agreed to deliver up all arms except what he needed for his personal use; that the Scotch Highlanders should do the same. He was asked to give up all property intended for the Indians that the patriots might divide the same among them, but he denied having any. Sir John was liberated on parole with the agreement that he was to go no farther west than the Flats, but east and south as far as he might choose, but not to go to any seaport town.

The amount of ammunition and arms was exceedingly small, and it turned out that Connell was an impostor. Schuyler had much trouble to preserve order in such a collection of undisciplined militia. Sir John did not keep his word but either directly or indirectly used his influence to excite the Indians to hostilities.

Schuyler learning this sent Colonel Dayton with a part
of a regiment to arrest him. But when the Colonel arrived at the Hall he found that Sir John with a large
number of his retainers and some disaffected loyalists
were on their way to Canada. Dayton examined all
the papers that he could find among Sir John's effects
and took Lady Johnson a prisoner to Albany. Stone
tells us there is some reason for thinking that a party
of Mohawks was sent from Canada to bring Sir John
out of the neighborhood of Johnstown. Be this as it
may, he and his followers reached Canada in a sorry
plight. For fear of falling in with the patriots he was
obliged to strike through the forests where he was
much delayed in the tangled underbrush. One by one
members of the party became exhausted and were left
to be brought in by Indians engaged in the British service. When they were once more united, they were
formed into a company under Sir John as Colonel in
the British army and were known as the "Royal
Greens." Tories fleeing to Canada were added to this
company from time to time. This partisan band was
actuated by such hatred of their old neighbors that
they performed some of the most dastardly deeds ever
committed by any body of civilized men.

In the latter part of the year 1775 Brant went to
England, doubtless to see for himself the strength of
the mother country, before committing himself to a
policy that might be the ruin of his nation if the patriots should win. It is thought by Stone that Guy
Johnson accompanied him on this voyage. He received
marked attention from all classes and promised as head
man of the nation to enlist 3000 Iroquois warriors in
the British cause. He returned by way of New York
and made a journey as best he could through a hostile
population to Canada. He took the field on his arrival and was present at the unfortunate affair of the

"Cedars" where Major Butterfield made his cowardly surrender.

The Continental Congress continued their efforts to win over the Indians and met a deputation of them at Philadelphia when an Onondaga Chief conferred upon President Hancock the name of the "Great Tree." In Spark's Life of Washington we read that Congress finally decided to enlist the Indians in the patriot cause, and offered a reward for every British officer that they might bring in. General Schuyler was strongly opposed to this resolution saying that the Indians could not be relied upon in a time of pressing emergency. From "time immemorial" the Great Council Fire at Onondaga had been kept brightly burning, but for some reason never known to historians it was extinguished, according to Stone, either in the last part of 1776 or in January of 1777. At the time many Onondaga warriors perished together with two principal Sachems. Perhaps the only reliable information which we have of this event so momentous to the Six Nations is found in an old letter among the papers of General Herkimer.

During the middle of the year 1777 a band of Mohawks led by their chief went to Unadilla and asked for food, saying that if it were not given them they would take it by force. They declared themselves in favor of the Great King. This showed the settlers what they had to fear and they began to collect at Cherry Valley and some of the older settlements. Brant was collecting his forces at Oghkwaga, so General Herkimer determined to march a small company to this place evidently with the determination of learning Brant's intentions. He was told by this cunning leader that the Indians were pledged to the King and that as the Indians had formerly fought the whites united they had nothing to fear now that the whites were quarreling among themselves. After this con ference Brant united his forces with those of Johnston and Butler. One of his first expeditions was to go to Cherry Valley with the hopes of making captures of prominent persons. But the place appeared to be fortified so the Indians laid in ambush near a bend in the road where they were concealed in the thick undergrowth. In the evening they waylaid and scalped Lieut. Wormwood, who had just borne dispatches to Cherry Valley, and took his companion prisoner. The dispatches which fell into the hands of Brant deceived him as to the real strength of the place and he retired without doing any more injury.

## SIEGE OF FORT SCHUYLER.

As the summer advanced rumors came to the settlements that Colonel St. Leger was at Oswego collecting a large force of Tories and Indians to capture the forts and to destroy the crops and buildings in the Mohawk valley and then unite with Burgoyne in the vicinity of Albany. He had with him the Royal Greens of Sir John and nearly 1000 Indians under Brant. He followed the old route up the Oswego river to the junction of the Seneca and Oneida to the lake, and along wood creek to Fort Stanwix. Before reaching here his force was augmented by other bodies of Indians, principally Cayugas and Onondagas. The fortress was in a dilapidated condition and was commanded by one of the bravest officers in the whole patriot army, colonel Gansevoort, with Colonel Willett second in command. The latter had just been sent to the help of this weak position. St. Leger, on marching from the forest into the clearing arranged his line of march so as to make the greatest possible display of his troops, hoping thus to frighten the little garrison. He had not yet learned that the American soldier is not frightened by mere display. The British Colonel made the investment complete. He placed his artillery

on the south; Sir John's followers occupied one bank
of the Mohawk while the Indians prowled through
the adjoining forests watching every avenue. Death
was certain to every one venturing many yards outside of the works. Even children who happened to
be captured were inhumanly treated. St. Leger issued a pompous proclamation which affected neither
the settlers nor the garrison. His artillery was able to
do but little damage. The garrison had provisions
sufficient for six weeks, and ammunition for their small
arms, but were sadly deficient in cannon. For a flag
they sewed together strips of white shirts, and blue
from a captured cloak, while the red was made up from
odds and ends found about the fort. What they lack-
ed in equipment they made up in courage, resolved to
hold out to the last well knowing that to surrender
was to die the most cruel death that the savage could
devise.

When the news reached the settlements that St.
Leger was about to start on his march toward the east
consternation seized upon all. But when he began to
approach Fort Stanwix their courage returned and
they responded readily to the call for volunteers to go
to the aid of Colonel Gansevoort. The country turned
out almost to a man, and Herkimer soon found himself at the head of nearly 1000 troops all eager to push
on to Fort Stanwix. Ariving at Oriskany a messenger
was sent forward to apprise Gansevcort that succor
was at hand. His arrival at the fort was to be announced by three successive discharges of cannon.
The message was delayed till late the following morning and General Herkimer did not think it prudent to
advance until re-inforcements came up; besides he
wished to act in conjunction with Colonel Willett who
was to make a sortie from the works. Brant had
learned that Herkimer was on his way to relieve Fort

Stanwix, and, knowing the country between that place and Oriskany he called into requisition all his knowledge of Indian warfare and of lying in ambush. The lay of the land was exactly suited to this sort of fighting. About two miles from Oriskany where the road crossed the river there was a swamp on either hand crossed by a causeway. Above the swamp were hills crowned with virgin forests. Here Brant skillfully hid his Indians in a semi-circle and waited for Herkimer and his men.

While Herkimer was waiting for re-inforcements or, at least knowledge that a sortie had been made from the besieged fort, his officers became eager to press forward. In vain the staunch old general urged the propriety of delaying. High words ensued. Many of the officers accused him of disloyalty, some even calling him a Tory and a coward. Herkimer retorted by telling them they would be the first to run should they suddenly meet the enemy. At last, losing his patience, he gave the order to "march on." The troops rushed forward in files two deep with an advance guard and flankers on either side. All unconscious of danger the van guard entered the ambuscade when suddenly the entire forest seemed alive with savages. Blood curdling yells sounded on every hand, and almost immediately the circle was completed in the rear cutting off all retreat.

Colonel Vischer's regiment and the baggage train were just entering the ravine, when, hearing the firing they fled leaving their companions to their fate. They were pursued by the Indians for a long distance and many of them either captured or killed, a just retribution to a command and its leader who would desert companions in a time of great peril. They fulfilled Herkimer's prophecy of a few hours before, and paid the penalty of their cowardice. Herkimer's men fell

around him like autumn leaves before a gale. His
horse was shot under him and his leg was shattered by
the same ball that killed his horse. At almost the
same time Colonel Cox and two of the captains fell
mortally wounded. From nearly every tree darted an
Indian to tomahawk and scalp the wounded. Amid
this scene of carnage, which promised the utter extermination of his army, Herkimer preserved his usual
self control. Seated on his saddle, with his back
against a tree, this heroic Dutchman calmly smoked
his pipe and gave orders for the conduct of the battle.
The battle raged thus for some time when the enemy
made a charge. Never was a charge withstood under
more trying circumstances, and never was greater courage displayed than these farmer soldiers showed at that
time. Both sides fought like tigers while above the
din of battle sounded the dreadful yell of the Indians.
The provincials were fighting for their homes and
their country. Suddenly a heavy shower broke upon
the combatants and arrested the progress of the fight.
During the lull the patriots arranged themselves on
more advantageous ground, placing two men behind a
tree instead of one man as heretofore. When the
action first began it was observed that whenever a man
fired his gun, before he could re-load, an Indian would
dart forward and tomahawk him. Under the new dis-
position one man reserved his fire much to the disad-
vantage of the Indian who attempted his former tactics.
Disgusted with this mode of fighting, and suffering
great loss of numbers, the Indians were about to with-
draw from the fight when they were re-inforced by
Major Watts with a detachment of the Royal Greens.
Many of these were acquaintances and neighbors of the
militia who sprang forward to meet this new foe, while
the pent up hatred of these neighbors showed itself in
one of the fiercest hand to hand fights recorded in the

annals of American History. Stone tells us "that
they fought each other with knives, some even dying
in each others embrace." At this time a firing was
heard in the direction of the fort. Colonel Butler
hearing it seized the opportunity to deceive the Provincials, by sending toward them a company of the
Royal Greens who wore caps similar to those worn by
the militia. At first the Provincials did not see their
green coats and thought that help was at hand, but on
a nearer approach the ruse was discovered and the
fight was again renewed. One of the militiamen was
so much deceived that he went up to shake hands with
one of the tories, a neighbor whom he supposed was a
friend. He was instantly taken prisoner, but in the
struggle which followed, another militiaman rushed
forward and struck down his captor and freed him.
This second man was then attacked by three of the
Tories who felled him to the ground. He received
two severe bayonet wounds, yet he succeeded in drag-
ging one of these men down upon him, when the pros-
trate Provincial stabbed the Tory, who was uppermost,
in the side, while others came and rescued the gallant
patriot from his assailants. Such was the struggle between old neighbors and acquaintances.

The Tories and Indians finding their numbers de-
pleted, and hearing fighting in the rear suddenly retreated leaving the Provincials masters of the field.

As soon as the heavy shower would permit, Colonel
Willett with two hundred and fifty volunteers rushed
from the fort and attacked the camp of Sir John. So
sudden and unexpected was the rush that Sir John did
not even have time to put on his coat which he had
taken off because of the heat. Colonel Willett and his
men drove the Tories at the point of the bayonet out
of their camp and across the Mohawk. They captured
several wagon loads of camp equipage which

they sent back to the fort. Stone says "among the spoils were clothing, blankets, stores, five British standards and the baggage of Sir John, with all of his papers." The Provincials swept through the camp of the Mohawks and returned to the fort without the loss of a man.

Thus ended one of the most fiercely contested battles of the Revolution. Schoolcraft gives the number of Indians slain as one hundred, thirty-six of whom were Senecas. This tribe had been induced to join in the expedition by a liberal use of liquor and promises that they were not to fight but to look on and smoke their pipes while the others did the fighting. But at the battle of Oriskany they found themselves in a position where they were "compelled to fight for their lives; and in the end of the battle were completely beaten with a great loss of killed and wounded." The narrative of Mary Jemison says that, when they returned to their towns and reported their great losses, "the mourning was excessive and was expressed by the most doleful yells, shrieks, howlings, and by inimitable gesticulations."

The unfortunate prisoners were the first with their blood to administer to their spirit of revenge. Indeed it was common report that the British officers connived at, if they did not consent to the most cruel and barbarous massacres of many prisoners.

After the battle General Herkimer's troops made litters upon which they carried many wounded comrades down the river to their homes. General Herkimer was conveyed to his home below Little Falls where he died a few days later from an unskillful amputation of his leg. Thus passed away one of the truest patriots of his day, a man whom the struggling patriots could ill afford to lose. "If Socrates died like a philosopher, and Rousseau like an unbelieving sentimentalist, General Herkimer died like a Christian hero."

After the Battle of Oriskany St. Leger used all the means at his command and that his cunning could devise to induce the garrison to surrender. He compelled Colonel Bellinger and Major Frey, who were prisoners in his camp, to write a letter to Colonel Gansevoort greatly exaggerating the loses in the battle of Oriskany, and that in all probability Burgoyne was already in Albany. This letter, having no apparent effect on the intrepid colonel, was followed by a verbal message from St. Leger stating in effect that if the garrison was not surrendered at once the Indians would be permitted to satisfy their revenge upon them as soon as the works were captured. Not only that, but the entire Mohawk valley would be ravaged with fire and sword. The messenger was emphatically informed that such a message was a degrading one for a British officer to send and one which no cultured officer would carry. Failing in this St. Leger issued ,an appeal to the residents of Tryon county urging them to accept proposals of peace and to use their influence to induce the garrison to surrender. If this were not done, that their homes and property would be destroyed, themselves carried into captivity and the entire garrison would be killed. Messengers were sent down the valley with this appeal. The anxiety displayed by St. Leger to induce a surrender convinced the besieged that the British doubted their ability to capture the place, and made them more determined to hold out. Colonel Willett, accompanied by a single officer, one dark night passed stealthily through the camps of Tories and Indians and made his way down the valley to General Schuyler's headquarters. At Fort Dayton he learned that General Schuyler had ordered General Arnold to go to the relief of Colonel Gansevoort. He proceeded to Albany and returned within a few days with the followers of General Arnold.

The messengers of St. Leger who had been dispatched down the valley with the appeal already mentioned stopped with a Tory not far from the present site of Herkimer. Here one night while at a secret meeting of Tories they were discovered and captured. Among the rest was Walter Butler who was in the act of making a speech to the assembly when he was arrested. At a subsequent court martial he received a death sentence, but, at the intercession of acquaintances, he was sent to prison in Albany from which he escaped later and became one of the most cruel leaders in that border war.

Living near Little Falls was a gypsy-like character who was the mother of an idiotic Tory by the name of Hon-yost Schuyler. The latter was one of the captured party spoken of above and had also received the sentence of death. When his mother heard of his danger she hastened to General Arnold's headquarters and pleaded eloquently for her son's life. The general yielded to her importunities on condition that Hon-yost would cut holes in his clothes to make it appear that he had had a narrow escape from the Patriots, and spread the report among St. Leger's troops that a large army was rapidly approaching for the relief of the garrison. A friendly Oneida Indian was selected to aid him in this enterprise, while the condemned Tory's brother was retained as a hostage to make sure that Hon-yost would carry out the plans. Hon-yost and the Oneida approached the camp from different directions for the purpose of confirming each others report. Hon-yost happened upon a body of Indians at just about the time they were holding a pow-wow to ascertain what would be their future luck in the campaign. In a very mysterious manner he imparted to

them the news that Arnold was within a few hours
march with a large army, "as numerous as the leaves
of the trees." From another direction came the
Oneida bearing a belt to the Indians, and confirming
all that Hon-yost had said, but adding that the army
was coming to attack the British and not the Indians.
Ever since the battle of Oriskany the Indians had
shown great dissatisfaction, and a vague rumor was all
that was needed to cause them to desert. In vain did
St. Leger assemble their chiefs and urge them to remain. Band after band moved away. The British
leaders began to quarrel among themselves, when an
old chief raised the cry "They are coming!" Away
went the Red Coats, officers and privates alike. Tents
were left standing, arms and knapsacks were thrown
away, and even much of their provisions, artillery and
ammunition were left.to be secured by the colonists.
The Indians not only enjoyed the confusion into which
they had thrown St. Leger and his troops, but they
fell upon the small detachments of British soldiers and
prisoners removed from the main body and murdered
them in cold blood.

St. Leger hastened back to Oswego and thence to
Montreal and later to Lake Champlain to aid Burgoyne. The Tory Hon-yost returned to Fort Dayton
and secured the release of his brother. Not many
months afterwards he left the country and joined the
forces of Sir John Johnson. After the close of the
war he returned to the Mohawk valley where he was
long known for the part which he played in the relief
of Fort Stanwix, as well as for his peculiarities.

#### RUMORS OF INDIAN AND TORY RAIDS.

Early in the fall of 1777 the colonists in the Mohawk,
Schoharie and Cherry valleys were greatly alarmed by
a report that Johnson and Butler were engaged in raising an army to desolate all these disaffected regions.

Later a messenger arrived at Canajoharie and announced that Johnson had engaged the services of twenty-two Indian nations against the Colonists. A belt was sent to the Oneidas to join with them, but if they refused they were to be the first to feel the effects of the invasion. In a measure to offset these rumors and messages an address was sent to the Six Nations with a view to win them to neutrality, if nothing more. But the poverty of the country and the lack of presents from Congress more than counterbalanced any good that may have come from the message. The British with an eye to business kept the Indians supplied with just the things to suit their needs and fancies. These appealed to the Indian much more strongly than logic or oratory.

### COUNCIL AT JOHNSTOWN.

The year 1777 opened with still more extended rumors of the union of the great western tribes with those of the Six Nations against the colonists. A council was called to convene at Johnstown some time in February to which were invited representatives of all the Iroquois. There was a large gathering of Oneidas, Onondagas and Tuscaroras, but the Mohawks and Cayugas sent a very small number, while the Senecas sent a message of surprise saying, "That while our tomahawks were sticking in their heads, their wounds bleeding and their eyes streaming with tears for the loss of friends at German Flatts, (Oriskany,) the commissioners should think of inviting them to a treaty."

The Oneidas and Tuscaroras convinced the commissioners of the sincerity of their friendship, but it was evident that the remaining Six Nations were wholly under the influence of British pay and presents. Indeed the Oneidas secretly told them that these Indians were under the control of Butler and would re-

new hostilities in the spring. It was at the time of
this council that it was proposed to erect a fort at
Cherry Valley. During the year before, three small
forts had been erected in the Schoharie valley. At
the request of the Oneidas it was also ordered to erect
a fort in their territory.

### RAID IN THE MOHAWK VALLEY

In the early part of the summer a large party of
Tories, who had previously fled to Canada, returned
and secured their families and considerable of their mov-
able property and returned by way of the Sacondaga and
Lake Champlain to Quebec. They picked up several
prisoners on their way and destroyed considerable
property.

### RAID IN SCHOHARIE VALLEY

At the opening of this same spring Brant returned
to his old quarters near Unadilla, while he himself perhaps did not murder helpless women and children, yet
his active mind planned excursions that were carried
out in all their horrid details, and yet the Tories were
oftentimes more cruel than the Indians. The historian
Stone quotes the following story in support of the
above story. "While a party of hostiles were prowling about the borders of Schoharie, the Indians killed
and scalped a mother, and a large family of children.
They had just completed the work of death, when
some loyalists of the party came up and discovered an
infant breathing sweetly in its cradle. An Indian
warrior, noted for his barbarity, approached the cradle
with his uplifted hatchet. The babe looked up in his
face and smiled; the feelings of nature triumphed over
the ferocity of the savage; the hatchet fell with his
arm, and he was about stooping down to take the in-
nocent in his arms, when one of the loyalists, cursing
him for his humanity, thrust it through with his
bayonet, and, thus transfixed, held it up struggling in

the agonies of death, as he exclaimed—"this too, is a rebel."

## BRANT BURNS SPRINGFIELD

It was in this year (1778) that Brant made a descent upon Springfield and captured all the men that he could find in the place and burnt the entire settlement, save one house in which he left the helpless women and children. A little later a large party of Indians were engaged with the Schoharie militia. They were victorious and carried away a large amount of plunder, and what they could not use they destroyed. But cruelty was not always with the Indians and Tories. The first blood shed in the beautiful Schoharie valley in this war was that of an old Sachem who was cruelly murdered by a band of Americans.—[Stone.]

# CHAPTER XIV

## THE WYOMING MASSACRE

Much has been written and said concerning the devastation of the beautiful Wyoming Valley; some claiming that the Tories were largely the cause of the raid and massacre; some that the celebrated Indian leader, Brant was the prime mover and instigator; others even going so far as to claim that the Provincialists foolishly accepted a challenge to meet the enemy half way. The following account of the battle is taken largely from facts collected by that indefatigable searcher after historical data, Stone.

For a great many years there had been a contention between land specalators and settlers as to who had the best claim to the land. At just about the time of the opening of the Revolution another of these bitter feuds sprang up engendering great factional hatred at the time that the people should have been united against the common foe. Many of the settlers who were loyalists fled from the valley, declaring that they would be revenged upon the whigs. Early in the summer of '78 they conducted John Butler with more than a thousand other Tories and Indians into this valley. Many of the able bodied men were away to the seat of war, leaving only a small company of soldiers, old men and boys to oppose this large force. The most of the women and children were assembled at Fort Forty. The Patriot leader attempted to surprise the Tories at Fort Wintermoot, but they had been apprised of the movement and were prepared. The Tories occupied the right and the Indians the left. The battle raged furiously for some time when the Patriots were commanded to fall back into a better position. The order was mistaken for a retreat and a panic ensued. This was the opportunity looked for by the Tories to revenge themselves upon their neighbors. Aided by the Indians they fell upon the fleeing Patriots and slaughtered without mercy. The Seneca Indians were rewarded with nearly two hundred and fifty scalps. A few escaped to the mountains. Darkness came and lent its horrors to the scene. The unfortunate prisoners were put to the greatest tortures. A party of them were bound while a half breed woman named Queen Esther murdered them with club and tomahawk. The inmates at Fort Forty, who had passed the night in the greatest apprehension, surrendered on the following morning to Butler with a strong promise that their persons and property should be safe. But no sooner had the British leader left the valley than the Indians who loitered behind began an indiscriminate massacre of the few remaining settlers. Some escaped to the mountains and made their way back to Connecticut. Others perished in a nearby swamp. Not a building was left standing. Crops, fences, fruit trees, in short everything that would gladden the eye of the colonists or supply the necessities of life was laid waste. Lossing says "The details of the desolation of the beautiful Wyoming valley and of the horrors of the flight of the survivors of the massacre form one of the darkest chapters in human history." It so pleased the British Secretary that he praised the Indians for the part they played and proposed to direct a series of such raids against the several frontier settlements.

For a long time it was claimed by writers that Brant and his Mohawks were present at the massacre of Wyoming. This the Indian leader and his descendants have strenuously denied.

### RAID ON COBLESKILL

Some time in the spring of this year Brant with a large following of Tories and Indians fell upon Cobleskill and destroyed much property and many lives. Captain Patrick with a small band of Provincials attempted to stay their progress but were all killed or taken prisoners except four who though badly wounded, escaped.

### RAID IN SCHOHARIE VALLEY

Later in the summer a band of Tories and Indians went into the Schoharie valley and began to destroy property and kill and take prisoners those who came in their way. Colonel Vrooman, who commanded the little fortress at Schoharie, either could not, or dared not attempt to stay their progress. Colonel Harper, who happened to be in the fort, was not satisfied to see property and lives sacrificed without an effort made to prevent it. Alone he made his way through the bands of prowling Indians and reached Albany where he secured a company of soldiers to go to the relief of Schoharie settlers. Early the next morning the enemy were surprised by a sudden attack of cavalry and fled precipitately.

Later a scalping party of seven Indians entered this valley and made a prisoner of Mr. Sawyer. They marched several miles into the forest, and having bound their captive laid down to rest. Mr. Sawyer feigned sleep, and when his captives, tired with their long march, were in deep sleep, he worked the cords loose from his wrists, arose quietly to his feet, seized a tomahawk and killed six of the sleeping Indians while the seventh one escaped. He then returned to his home.

### RAID ON HERKIMER

In the early fall a scout by the name of John Helmer

came into the settlements near Forts Dayton and Herkimer with the news that Brant at the head of a large party of Indians was within a few miles and would be upon them during the night. The news spread rapidly and soon the excited settlers came hastening to the forts bringing their more valuable articles. They had no time to prepare for the protection of their grain and cattle. The night set in dark and rainy. Brant arrived at Shoemaker's place where he sheltered himself from the storm, hoping to take the settlers by surprise at dawn of the following day. In the gray light of the early morning the Indians scattered through the settlement and at a given signal the work of destruction began. Every where were to be seen flames arising from burning buildings and the dusky forms of the barbarians driving off horses and cattle.

The colonists looked out from Fort Herkimer and saw both his season's labor and winter's provisions disappear before the torch of the invader. Shortly after leaving with their plunder they were pursued by a body of militia, but to no purpose. A party of Oneida Indians however went to the Unadilla settlement, burnt several dwellings and recaptured considerable of the booty, besides taking prisoners.

SETTLERS INVADE THE INDIAN COUNTRY

There were stationed in the Schoharie valley several regular troops and a company of them determined to invade the territory of Brant. By a rapid march they entered Unadilla which they found deserted. They burned the entire settlement with the only saw mill on the river. They hastened to Brant's head quarters, Oghkwaga, which had also been hastily deserted. Here they found an abundance of provisions stored for winter use, with some cattle and furniture. They rested for a day or so and then proceeded to lay waste the entire section. They went further down the river and destroyed the Indian castle. The campaign lasted sixteen days and was one that required much courage and hardihood.

Walter Butler after his escape from confinement at Albany, went through the Seneca country on his way to Niagara. Burning with thoughts of revenge he stirred up the ill feelings of the Senecas and succeeded in raising a war party with which to desolate the frontier settlements in retaliation for his recent indignities. On the way he met Brant whom he induced to return with his Mohawks, making a total force of nearly seven hundred men.

### MASSACRE AT CHERRY VALLEY

The fort which had been recently built at Cherry Valley was commanded by a man not much versed in Indian warfare. He was told that a large party of rangers and Indians were on the march against his post but he refused to believe it, saying that it was only an idle rumor. The people urged him to permit them to move their effects into the fort, but he allayed their fears, and sent out a scouting party to watch for any approaching enemy. These scouts made a considerable journey into the forest, and wearied with their day's march, kindled a bright fire and lay down to rest. When they awoke they found themselves prisoners compelled to furnish information to their captors as to the strength and location of the fort and principal families of the settlement. Having secured all necessary information, they pushed on to within a mile of the village where they halted for the night concealed by the thick evergreens. Early in the morning a traveler rushed into the settlement and warned the commander that a large band of Indians was approaching. Even then he was incredulous until the Indians burst upon the settlement, and the work of

death began. Whole families were killed or taken
prisoners. One household were killed while at family
prayers. It is asserted that in many instances the
Tories were more cruel than the Indians, and that a
chief of the Mohawks interposed to protect the helpless. One man, while working in the field, saw the
Indians between himself and his house. He fled to
the woods and thus escaped. When he returned to
his house he found it on fire and his wife and three
children killed. Men who had been away from home
on business returned to find their property destroyed,
homes in ashes, and their loved ones either murdered
or carried into captivity.

Butler and Brant with their captives and plunder,
marched a long distance into the forests when it was
decided to send back the women and children, except
such as it was thought best to retain to effect an advantageous exchange of prisoners. Campbell in his
annals of Tryon county tells us that not a single building was left in the settlement. All the stores and
provisions were destroyed, and hardly a living creature
remained except the few soldiers in the fort, which the
Indians were not brave enough to capture. This post
was deserted and the valley was a scene of desolation
until peace came, when the survivors of that terrible
struggle returned and rebuilt their homes, and culti
vated their neglected farms.

# CHAPTER XV

### THE PATRIOTS INVADE THE ONONDAGA COUNTRY

The early spring of the year 1779 was made memorable by a campaign against the Onondagas. This tribe had pursued a vacillating policy, pretending at times to be friendly toward the cause of the Colonists, but nearly always working with the British. Rumors of an intended invasion by Brant, who was to be aided by the Onondagas convinced the authorities at Albany that the time had come when this tribe should be treated as enemies; so an expedition was secretly planned which set out in the fog of an April morning and hastened by way of Oneida Lake to their territories.

The Indians lived in a series of villages along the Onondaga creek and had for many years kept the national council fire burning. Arriving at the edge of the village the Provincials separated into several companies in order the better to take by surprise the different villages. But in some unknown manner the wily foe had learned of the approach of an enemy, and fled leaving everything behind. But few captives were taken, while a very large quantity of provisions were destroyed, and many guns and rifles were captured. Their council house and three entire villages were burned, and their horses and cattle were killed. It is a disputed point in the history of these times whether the Onondagas merited such chastisement. But when we call to mind the raids that had been made by the Tories and Indians upon defenceless settlements, and that many of the patriot soldiers had lost friends and relatives in these midnight raids, we wonder at the clemency they showed in their treatment of the Indians who fell into their power.

The Oneidas, who had been uniformly on the side of the Patriots, or at least neutral in the quarrel, were greatly excited over the treatment which their neighbors, the Onondagas, had received, and sent a messenger to ask the cause. It was explained to them that parties from that nation were constantly on the war path and that scalps were found in their castles. If these reasons were not satisfactory they should appeal to the commissioners at Albany. It does not appear that the Oneidas followed up the matter any further, and there it dropped.

### DESCENT UPON PALATINE AND STONE ARABIA.

At the same time that the expedition was being made against the Onondagas, a small party of western Indians entered Palatine where they captured a few prisoners and drove the frightened people into the fort. Seizing several horses they made good their escape. A party of Mohawks made a descent upon Stone Arabia, burned several houses and put to death a number of the inhabitants. A wandering party of the western Iroquois also entered the Schoharie settlements and marched away with prisoners and plunder. So many incursions at various points at the same time created great consternation and an urgent appeal was made to General Clinton for help. Within a short time a large force was marched up the Mohawk, much to the relief of the settlers.

### THE ONONDAGAS SEEK REVENGE

It is not to be supposed that a strong and warlike nation would be frightened into submission at the loss of property and villages. The loss of the ancient council fire called forth threats of dire vengeance, and within a short time three hundred of their fiercest warriors were on their way to the east determined to wipe out their recent disgraces in the blood of the hated pale face. Their intentions evidently were to fall upon Cobleskill and capture it by surprise. But the inhabitants, having been warned, sent to Schoharie for aid, and soon a detachment of continental troops were on their way. On the following morning a small band of Indians were seen in the edge of the clearing. Nearly the whole force was sent out to give them battle. The Indians retreated into the forest and thus drew the Provincials into an ambush. Suddenly the terrible war whoop sounded on every hand. From every tree darted forth an Indian with the deadly tomahawk and scalping knife. Those who escaped fled with the panic stricken inhabitants to the Schohariekill. Many more of the latter would have perished had not a few braver than the rest entered a house on the road and held the Indians at bay for some time. The Onondagas were unable to dislodge them, so they set fire to the building and the brave soldiers perished in the flames. The entire settlement was destroyed, and more than twenty were killed or taken prisoners. The Indians, doubtless feeling that they had been amply revenged, returned in great triumph to their homes.

## MASSACRE AT MINISINK

Before the close of the year the ever restless Brant planned another attack upon the exposed settlements. This time the blow fell upon Minisink in Orange county. At the head of a small band of his Mohawks and a few Tories, who were acquainted with the county, he stole upon the sleeping settlement and set many of the houses on fire before the inhabitants realized that an enemy was near. Several months before the soldiers formerly stationed there had been removed, leaving the settlement without protection. Panic stricken they fled from their burning homes, leaving the invaders to riot upon the spoils. They arrived in Goshen in a pitiable plight. Nearly all had rushed from their homes with little or no preparation for such a journey.

The entire settlement was laid waste, crops were destroyed and cattle driven away, and several people were killed or taken prisoners. Brant and his small body of followers took what booty they could carry and joined the main body of his army.

Colonel Tusten, who was then at Goshen, set out in pursuit of the enemy with about one hundred and fifty men. When he learned the number of Brant's followers, he called a council of war and advised not attacking the enemy until reinforcements could be obtained. But the majority would not listen to prudence and the march was immediately resumed. They overtook Brant near the mouth of Lackawaxen creek. Through some lack of tactics the Continentals became separated and the Mohawk leader wheeled his men into the gap and closed in upon the main body. The Patriots fought like demons but were overwhelmed by numbers and nearly all killed. When the order was given to retreat a panic ensued and the Indians fell upon them and tomahawked all within their reach, not even sparing the wounded or the attending surgeons. Only thirty escaped of all the number that had so proudly left their homes but a short time before bent on revenge.

Many years afterward the bones of the slain were gathered and buried and a neat marble slab was erected bearing the names of the victims. In 1862, through the generosity of Dr. Cash, a neat monument was erected comemorative of that sad affair.

# CHAPTER XVI

## REV. SAMUEL KIRKLAND.

Any work touching the history of the Six Nations would be incomplete without, at least, a short account of the most famous missionary among the Iroquois, one who did-more than any other white man to preserve the friendship of the Oneida and Tuscarora Clans for the Patriots during their long struggle for political freedom.

Rev. Samuel Kirkland was well fitted by nature for a missionary among the Indians. He had great constitutional strength, and was vivacious, courageous and benevolent. Devoted to the cause of the Indian, he labored with all the powers of a great and noble mind for his conversion. He first went among the Senecas, where he remained a year and a half. He made friends among them, but few if any converts. Unable to accomplish much among these tribes, he returned east and established Joseph Wooley as a teacher among the Mohawks. They went by way of Cherry Valley to the famous Indian village of Onohogkwage, where they received a hearty welcome. The Mohawks were delighted to have a teacher among them, and they promised Mr. Kirkland to take good care of Wooley, after which the missionary returned to Johnson Hall, where he remained till mid-winter. Here he made preparations to return to the Seneca country.

Accompanied by two Seneca Indians, he set out on snow shoes with a forty pound pack of clothing and books to traverse that long and perilous trail. Unaccustomed to such severe exertions, he soon began to feel the effects of the journey. His guides went ahead and made a snow shoe road for him. At night they

would clean away the deep snow and make a fire, near
which a bed was made of evergreen boughs. As they
travelled farther west, his sufferings from swollen feet
and ankles caused by walking on snow shoes, were severe, and he must have perished had it not been for the
kindness of his guides. At the principal Oneida village, he remained a short time till he was able to re-
sume his journey. At Onondaga he was glad to again
accept the hospitality of the Indians, who assembled
at their Council house to hear the message of Sir William to the Senecas. Mr. Kirkland took special pains
to record that "the Council house was 80 feet long and
contained four fires. The messenger made a speech
for three quarters of an hour, and was responded to by
the head Sachem, who spoke for an hour like Demos-
thenes." After the Council broke up, there was much
hand shaking when the party started again late at night
on their journey to the Seneca country. Twenty-three
days after leaving Johnson Hall, foot sore, and almost
exhausted, he arrived at Kanadasegea, the Capital of
the Seneca Nation. After discussing the matter in
two different Councils he was finally adopted by the
head Sachem and placed in a small family. Shortly
afterward his host suddenly died. This placed Mr.
Kirkland in a perilous position, but he finally won the
confidence of the Indians. After some time a famine
occurred and he determined to set out for Johnson Hall
for provisions. He was accompanied by a Seneca with
his squaw. They nearly lost their lives on Oneida
Lake during a severe storm, but finally reached the
Hall where the Indian woman died, greatly mourned
by her husband.

The missionary seems to have been able to accomplish but little among the Senecas. It is to be regret-
ted that Mr. Kirkland did not write fully concerning

the life of these people at that time. It would have given us much historical information which now can not be obtained. In the summer of 1766, he began his work among the Oneidas, which he continued for forty years. Here he built him a home and associated with him in his work, David Fowler and his wife, two educated Indians. In 1769, he went to New England, where he married Miss Jerusha Bingham, a niece of Dr. Wheelock. Mrs. Kirkland was a great help to her husband and exerted a marked influence over the Oneida women.

When it became evident that there was to be a rupture with the mother country, Mr. Kirkland travelled from tribe to tribe using his influence to preserve the neutrality of the Indians. To what extent he succeeded has already been mentioned. For about two years the Oneidas and Tuscaroras kept out of the fight, but later they rallied under the leadership of the celebrated Oneida chief—Skenando, and did excellent service for the patriot cause.

This popular chief was a great friend of Mr. Kirkland, and one of the wisest councillors the Six Nations ever had. He died at the age of 110, and was buried at Clinton, N. Y., in an orchard on the old Kirkland homestead. After the Revolution the missionary set about to repair the ravages of war, collect the scattered families and rebuild their homes. Mrs. Kirkland died in 1788, and it was about this time that Mr. Kirkland wrote an account of the Six Nations.

In 1791, he married Miss Mary Donnelly who died in Clinton in 1839, aged 84. One daughter married Mr. J. H. Lathrop, of Utica; another Mr. Francis Amory, of Boston, and a third Dr. Edward Robinson, a professor of Hamilton College.

Mr. Kirkland made great efforts to found a school at

Clinton, and finally secured a charter for Hamilton, Oneida Academy. He gave a large tract of land and set apart 12 acres as a site for a school. This commands an extensive view of the valley and village and is now covered with a great variety of trees and shrubs, with class memorials and modern educational buildings, making it one of the pleasantest college sites to be found. Here is also preserved the little, old house in which the great missionary lived.

Mr. Kirkland died in 1808 and was buried in the land he helped to win to civilization, with his wife and daughter on one side and the "white man's friend," Skenando, on the other.

# CHAPTER XVII

## SULLIVAN'S CAMPAIGN

So frequent had been the forages of the Indians, which had always been conducted with much cruelty, that it was decided to make an expedition into the land of the Iroquois and "pay them off in their own coin."

Clinton was ordered to collect a large body of men at Schenectady, and transporting boats and provisions overland to the head of Otsego lake, to descend the Susquehanna and join Johnson at Tioga. The people along the Mohawk and in the adjoining sections responded nobly to the call for help, and in a few days the General was able to report 1500 men, nearly 200 boats and a large supply of provisions, so many indeed that General Washington declared that Clinton would be delayed and could not keep his movements secret from the Indians.

A large party of Oneidas had volunteered to join the expedition, but on receiving information that they would be attacked by the British unless they remained neutral they decided to remain at home, except such few as might individually wish to act as guides and runners.

While waiting at Otsego lake for orders from General Sullivan, Clinton caused the waters of the lake to be dammed up, thus enabling him to float his boats down the river when the proper time should arrive. He was kept impatiently waiting until near the middle of August by the slow movement of General Sullivan. When, at last, he received word to proceed down the river, he embarked his troops and supplies, and letting out the waters from the lake, was borne rapidly on the

swollen river toward the point of juncture with the
greater part of the expedition.   The few scattered
settlers and the Indians along the river were  surprised
to see their crops  swept  away  by  a  sudden  rise of
water in the river, and when the latter considered that
there had been no rain for a long time, they concluded
that the Great  Spirit  must  be  offended  with  them;
while the sight of a large flotilla of soldiers riding upon
the bosom of a river that had  never  floated  anything
larger than a birch  bark  canoe  struck  terror  to  the
bravest heart.

Sometime after  the  middle  of  August  the  united
commands, 5000 strong  commenced  their  westward
march  to  the  land  of  the Cayugas and Senecas.   So
long had General Sullivan been  making  his  preparations that  the  Indians  had  become  apprised  of  his
movements and had thrown up earthworks at Newton,
not far from the present site of Elmira.

### BATTLE OF NEWTON

The army marched with the greatest caution destroying everything on the route that might in any way aid
the Indians.   Late in the morning of the 29th the advance guard came upon the works of the enemy.
These had been so arranged  that  they  could  be  approached only in front and on the left flank which
rested upon a high ridge thickly covered with Indians,
back of which was another  ridge  also  well  guarded.
A skirmishing was kept up until the main body of  the
army arrived with General Sullivan.   He immediately
sent a brigade to carry the heights and turn the left
flank of the enemy while he engaged them in front.
Then was fought one of the most exciting  battles  recorded in Indian history.   The Indians fought for
their families,  their  lands  and  the  graves  of  their
fathers.   They  contested  the  ground  inch  by  inch,

springing like panthers from tree to tree, refusing to yield even at the point of the bayonet. Brant, the leader of the Indians, seeing that their left flank must not be turned at any cost, was everywhere present leading and cheering his men. The fearful battle cries of the Indians and the shrieks of the wounded were drowned by the thunder of the cannon in the valley below. In a last desperate attempt Brant brought a company of Johnson's Rangers to the help of his hard pressed followers, but too late. His left flank was turned, and the enemy fearing that Sullivan's men would get into their rear, raised their cry of retreat and fled from the field. So precipitate was their retreat that they could not carry away all their dead with them. Their loss in killed and wounded was much greater than that of the American army which sustained a loss of only six killed and less than 50 wounded. These together with the heavy artillery were sent back to Tioga, while the greater part of the army started westward in light marching order. Where-ever they came to buildings and growing crops they halted long enough to destroy them and then hurried on. Why the Indians did not oppose them at some of the narrow and difficult passes does not appear. In some places they were obliged to ford streams flanked by high hills where a few brave men could have delayed the progress of a large army.

In a short time they reached Katherine's town at the head of Seneca lake. · This they laid in ashes, and they destroyed crops and orchards leaving only a desolate waste.

### CONDITION OF THE SENECAS AND CAYUGAS

Much has been written both for and against Sullivan's expedition. The Cayugas and Senecas had reached a good degree of civilization. They had cleared large tracts of land on which they raised crops that would gladden the heart of any farmer. They had excellent orchards of apples, pears, and peaches. They had large towns and villages, many of them laid out in streets, and composed of framed houses, often painted, and containing many of the necessities of civilized life. The only advantage that the Americans could hope to attain by the destruction of these homes was to deprive the Indians of the means of subsistence for the coming winter and thus throw their support upon the British at Niagara.

### DESTRUCTION OF THE SENECA CAPITAL

Every where the terror stricken Indians fled before Sullivan's army. In a short time they reached the beautiful Seneca capital, Kanadaseagea, surrounded by large fields covered with crops and fruit orchards. The inhabitants had fled leaving their winter supplies, their orchards, the product of years of toil, their comfortable homes, to the mercies of a revengeful invader. Several towns in this locality were destroyed, and the army left in its track only scenes of destruction and devastation. The towns of Kanandaigua and Honeoye were wiped out together with great stores of grain, vegetables and fruit. From this place preparations were made to march upon Genesee, the large village of the tribe.

### BATTLE OF GENESEE.

Here the Indians placed their women and children out of reach of the Americans and prepared to defend their town. A sharp skirmish ensued when the Indians suddenly turned and fled. The soldiers were greatly pleased with the beauty and fertility of the Genesee valley. Sullivan in his report said "The town of Genesee contained 128 houses, mostly large and very elegant. It was beautifully situated, almost encircled with a clear flat, extending a number of miles, over which extensive fields of corn were waving, together with every kind of vegetable that could be conceived." After quoting the foregoing, the historian Stone goes on to say, "But the entire army was immediately engaged in destroying it, and the axe and the torch soon transformed the whole of that beautiful region from the character of a garden to a scene of drear and sickening desolation. Forty Indian towns, the largest containing 128 houses were destroyed. Corn, gathered and ungathered, to the amount of 160,000 bushels, shared the same fate; their fruit trees were cut down; and the Indians were hunted like wild beasts, till neither house, nor fruit tree, nor field of corn, nor inhabitant, remained in the whole country. The gardens were enriched with great quantities of useful vegetables, of different kinds. The size of the cornfields, as well as high degree of cultivation in which they were kept, excited wonder; and the ears of corn were so remarkably large, that many of them measured twenty inches in length. So numerous were the fruit trees, that in one orchard they cut down fifteen hundred." From this point General Sullivan seems to have turned back, retracing his steps over the devastated district to Tioga. On the route he sent detachments to the small villages and fields lying several miles from the main traveled road. On these raids 9 towns and villages, including the capital of the Cayugas, were destroyed, besides great quantities of provisions, and large numbers of fruit trees.

Why General Sullivan did not continue his journey to the seat of British power among the Indians at Niagara, from which Tory and Indian raids were so frequently made, has never been satisfactorily explained. Certainly this was one of the objects which the commander-in-chief had in view when he ordered the organization of the expedition. It could not have been because of the weakness of his army. He had fought no great battle, except at Newton, and his soldiers had enjoyed excellent health. Niagara was in no condition to withstand an attack, and had no time to bring reinforcements from Montreal or Quebec. Finally it could not be lack of provisions for his soldiers destroyed enough to have sustained an army many times its size during a much longer campaign. To be sure he brought the hardships of war home to those who had made so many raids against the white settlers; but instead of subduing them he only aroused them to a greater frenzy for revenge. Stone says "Stimulated by a yet keener thirst for revenge, clouds of savages were afterward again and again seen to sweep through the valley of the Mohawk with the scalping knife and the torch." And who can blame the red man then "driven from his beautiful country, his habitations laid in ruins, his fields laid waste, his orchards uprooted, his altars and the tombs of his fathers overthrown."

ARREST OF THE MOHAWKS AT THE LOWER CASTLE

When the Johnson's and other Tories influenced the Mohawks to accompany them to Canada, there was one clan which refused to accompany them. This clan lived at the Lower Castle on the Mohawk river, on terms of friendship with their white neighbors, preserving a strict neutrality. General Sullivan had been informed that these Indians were acting as spies and secretly aiding and encouraging those Tories and Indians who were making frequent raids into the Mohawk and Cherry Valleys.

On the return march he ordered Colonel Gansevoort to proceed down the Mohawk valley and capture the entire clan, burn their castle and carry them prisoners to Albany. When the Colonel arrived in the neighborhood of the castle he learned that the Indians were even then sheltering those white people who had recently been deprived of their homes by Indian and Tory raids. The inhabitants of the frontier begged him not to destroy the property of the clan, consisting of homes as convenient as many owned by the white settlers; of stores of provisions, and of cows horses and wagons. However the Colonel carried them all captives to Albany where General Schuyler procured their release.

# CHAPTER XVIII.

## DESTRUCTION OF THE ONEIDA CASTLE

The winter which followed the invasion of Sullivan has come down in history as one of the most severe known to have occurred on this continent. The Indians whose property had been destroyed were compelled to seek food and shelter of the British at Niagara. A great many fell sick, and not a few perished from hunger and exposure.

Some time during this winter the Indians and Tories made a raid against the Oneidas, destroyed their village and castle, and drove them down the Mohawk where the colonists settled them near Schenectady and supported them to the close of the war. Dr. Kirkland said that "this dispersion of the Oneidas, and the devastation of their country, were greatly detrimental to their nation. When the war came on, they had attained to some degree of regularity, industry, and prosperity. But, driven from their homes, reduced to want, dependence, and abject poverty, their habits became more intemperate and idle than ever, and they never recovered from their depression."

## RAID OF HARPERSFIELD

Brant, actuated by the strongest feelings of revenge on account of the sufferings of his people, began early in the spring to prepare for the destruction of the frontier settlements. Early in April at the head of a band of Tories and Indians he fell upon the settlement of Harpersfield and destroyed it, killing a few and taking several prisoners. He then set out through the forests toward the upper Schoharie fort. He suddenly fell in with a small band of militia who were engaged in making maple sugar while they kept watch for any straggling bands of the enemy. When busily engaged in their work they heard the appalling war whoop and the deadly crack of the rifle. Those who survived the first onslaught were taken prisoners. Brant was deceived into the belief that the fort had recently been strongly reinforced, and so he retraced his steps to Niagara. The journey was one of great peril to the prisoners, and Brant exerted himself to the utmost to save their lives from the revenge of his followers. Added to this all suffered extremely from the want of food. However, many of them lived through the terrible ordeal and finally returned to their desolate homes.

As spring advanced, and the snow disappeared, roving bands af Indians, often guided by Tories, fell upon the exposed settlements in all directions, even going as far south as Orange county.

### RAID ON LITTLE FALLS

One of these raids was made upon a settlement near what is now the village of Little Falls. The only important mills for grinding flour for several miles were situated at this place and owned by a Mr. Ellis. But few men were at the mills at the time and not prepared for an attack. They tried to escape, but most of them were taken prisoners, and the property was entirely distroyed.

### SIR JOHN JOHSON'S RAID INTO JOHNSTOWN

When the Johnsons left the country for Canada they left a large amount of treasure and several slaves at their old home at Johnstown. Sir John determined to secure these, and at the same time severely punish those whig neighbors who had been the cause of all his troubles. One dark night in early spring he entered Johnstown at the head of about 250 Tories and Indians, while a company of nearly the same number were sent to destroy all the dwellings along the

Mohawk except those belonging to Tories. The houses were plundered and burned and most of their inhabitants killed or made prisoners.

Sir John, avoiding the small garrison, marched to his old home, secured 20 slaves, and a large amount of treasure, which was carried away in the knapsacks of 40 soldiers. He collected also a band of loyalists, after which he united his forces and with his prisoners and booty returned unmolested to Canada. He wisely avoided the usual traveled routes and so the army sent by Governor Clinton was unable to capture his forces. When we consider that the entire country was panic stricken, and that the people cruelly murdered were tne old neighbors of Sir John, many of whom had rendered acts of kindness to himself and to different members of his family, we do not hesitate to place this act among the most cruel and bloodthirsty of that terrible border strife. Stone says, "The irruption, however, was one of the most indefensible aggressions upon an unarmed and slumbering people, which stain the annals of the British arms."

### BRANT DESTROYS CANAJOHARIE

On the summer following this incursion a large supply of provisions was to be sent to Fort Schuyler, and, as a rumor had been spread abroad that Brant was intending to capture these, all the militia around Canajoharie was called out to help protect the escort from attack. The wily Indian leader then fell upon the defenceless settlements and laid them waste. In Almon's Remembrancer we read "that in the Canajoharie settlement 99 buildings were burnt, 17 persons killed, and 52 taken prisoners. On the Schoharie 27 buildings burnt, 7 persons killed, and 21 taken prisoners. At Normanskill there were 20 houses burnt." "The forts destroyed by Brant at Canajoharie, were built by the people themselves, but had not yet been garrisoned. The inhabitants had complained bitterly that they were thus compelled to leave their own firesides unprotected, to assist the government in re-opening the communication with Fort Schuyler. But being assured that their town could be in no danger, they submitted to the order, and their militia marched to the upper section of the valley. The result was deplorable enough; while the success of his stratagem added another plume to the crest of the "The Great Captain of the Six Nations." (Stone.) Sir John Johnson and Brant, not satisfied with the excursions separately undertaken, determined to unite their forces and enter upon a campaign of destruction that would, if possible eclipse Sullivan's expedition.

### SIR JOHN AND BRANT UNITE TO DESTROY ALL THE VALLEY SETTLEMENTS

In the summer following the Johnstown expedition, Sir John collected a force composed of his Royal Greens, a number of Mohawks, a detachment of Butler's rangers, and a company of regulars and ascending the St. Lawrence he crossed over the country to the head waters of the Susquehanna where he united his forces with those of Brant and Cornplanter. They were provided with excellent arms and a large amount of ammunition, and according to the report of Mary Jemison, the Indians never went upon the war path vowing deeper vengeance against the usurpers of their hunting grounds. From the Susquehanna they crossed the hills to the Schoharie Valley. Silently passing the upper fort they began the work of destruction in the early dawn. Those in the middle fort were first apprised of the approach of the enemy by the sight of the burning buildings. The commandant sent out a company of volunteers, but they soon learned that they were opposed by a large body of Indians and Tories, when they quietly retreated. The fortress was quickly surrounded, and Sir John planted his little battery on a rise of ground commanding the place. A flag of truce was sent toward the fort but was fired upon by the intrepid Murphy of Schoharie fame. Thereupon Sir John began a brisk fire which did no special damage. After a time a second flag of truce was sent which was again fired upon by Murphy. When Sir John could find no other means of access to the fort he determined to take it by assault. Having arranged his men for that purpose he sent forward a third flag of truce which Murphy again drove back. All at once the Tories raised the siege and continued their march down the river, burning and plundering as they went. The crops were unusually large that year, and the settlers were entirely unprepared for such an invasion, consequently every thing known to belong to a Whig was totally destroyed, besides several killed and a large number taken prisoners. The historian Stone tells us that Sir John had ordered that the church at the middle fort should not be destroyed. How well his commands were obeyed is shown by the following quotation from a paper read by the Hon. Geo. L. Danforth at the centennial of the Old Dutch church at Middleburgh. "And now coming down to the terrible but glorious 17th day of October, 1780, terrible in its work of destruction and desolation, glorious in the perfect defence and triumphant resistance of the three forts—before the sun begins his career that day we hear the boom of the alarm gun at the upper fort 5 miles away, and the guns of our fort over there answer, aye, aye! We wait and watch in feverish suspense, and soon we see the advance down the valley of the British, Tories and Indians, working their way by smoke and flame. They reach Weiserdorf; and barns and dwellings, stacks of hay and straw, yield to the barbarous torch, and with an additional pang of sorrow, we see the lurid flames mount the sides and circle the steeple of the old Dutch meeting house, dear to the hearts of the heroic band who stand at the middle fort ready to receive, and able to roll back the shock and charge of the coming foe."

Farther down the valley Sir John divided his forces sending the Regulars down the valley while the Indians skirted the clearings along the foot of the range of hills at the left. They halted but a little while at the lower fort, and evidently not being courageous enough to make an assault, continued their work of devastation as far as Fort Hunter where they encamped for the night. There he remained long enough to send out small parties in all directions to destroy every piece of property that could be found and to secure prisoners. When the entire country had become a scene of desolation and waste he proceeded up the Mohawk completely destroying every thing on both banks of the river.

General Van Rensselaer hearing of the invasion of the Schoharie valley set out in pursuit. He camped but a few miles from Sir John's motley troop, but delayed long enough to allow a detachment of the enemy to branch off to the north to attack Fort Paris in Stone Arabia. This fortress was under the command of Colonel Brown who, by the direction of General Van Rensselaer, immediately marched with his small troop to meet the foe. But the general failed to co-operate with him and he and his brave followers were overpowered and many were killed. Those who escaped fled to Fort Plain. The scattered detachments of Sir John's troops continued their work of devastation gradually marching towards the west and collecting at a place called "Klock's Field." The enemy selected a field of battle so as to be protected on one side by the bend of the river. Sir John's immediate followers were placed in the front with Brant's Indians on the flank. The patriot army numbering now about 1500 men did not come up with the enemy until late in the afternoon when an attack was immediately made. The Indians were soon put to flight, but darkness coming on, the General would not allow a pursuit. The next morning Sir John had disappeared. One noted historian declares that had the Continental troops kept up the fight and pursuit for a short time they would have had the enemy completely hemmed in the bend of the river where they would have been obliged to surrender. The flying enemy were pursued rapidly as far as Fort Herkimer from which point General Van Rensselaer sent word to his advance guard of Oneidas and militia to continue the pursuit. The Oneida chief, finding himself in the rear of the flying enemy, and learning that he was not supported by the main part of the army turned back, and thus ended what might have been a glorious victory for the patriots had the campaign been conducted with more energy.

A small company had been sent from Fort Schuyler to destroy the boats which Sir John had left to convey his troops back to Oswego. Sir John surprised these, took them prisoners and proceeded on his way unmolested.

The winter which followed brought great distress to all the outposts of the north. The Indians and Tories had destroyed so many provisions the preceding autumn that the settlers could scarcely support their families. As a result they had but very little to send to the army. Brant kept warriors constantly watching the Mohawk valley so as to cut off supplies going west to Fort Schuyler. No one could travel except under a strong escort, without being captured by some band of roving Indians. During the late winter and early spring Brant captured a number of scouts and no small amount of provisions. Added to all this the Oneidas were no longer in a safe position, for Brant had shown great hatred toward them and was likely at any time to attempt their destruction.

The courage of the settlers had sunk to its lowest point by the repeated incursions of the Tories and Indians when Colonel Willett was appointed to the command of the militia for the defence of the country against the raids of the barbarians. Scarcely had he entered upon his command before he had an opportunity to display his abilities as an Indian fighter.

### DESTRUCTION OF CURRIETOWN

Early in the summer a band of Indians attacked and burned the settlement of Currietown and retreated to their night encampment in a dense forest. Colonel Willett quickly raised a band of volunteers and proceeded to surprise them while asleep, but found it impossible to reach them before daylight of the following morning. The Indians learning of their approach took a more favorable position and waited their appearance. A small number was sent in advance to draw out the Indians. They fled at the first fire followed by the main body of the enemy. These were met by the main body of Willett's men who poured in a deadly fire. At the same time the Indians tried to turn his right wing. Failing in both attempts they betook themselves to trees and attempted the usual Indian tactics. Soon the settlers cheered on by their gallant leader, chased the Indians out of the woods and down the Susquehanna at the point of the bayonet. Colonel Willett's loss of men was small while the Iroquois lost more than an eighth of the number engaged, besides all of their camp and plunder.

### LAST INVASION OF THE MOHAWK VALLEY.

It remains to record the last serious invasion of the Mohawk valley by the Tories and Indians. The Johnsons and their Tory neighbors were constantly moved by a great hatred toward the whig residents of the valley, and so were constantly planning for their destruction. In October of 1781 Major Ross assisted by Butler and his son suddenly appeared at Warrensbush near the junction of the Mohawk and Schoharie rivers and began the work of plundering and burning. They crossed the river not far from Tribe's Hill and marched rapidly towards Johnstown killing and taking Whig prisoners and destroying all their property. Colonel Willett, learning of the approach of the enemy, made every effort to collect the scattered militia. By a forced night march he reached Fort Hunter the following morning. Having forded the river he overtook the enemy not far from Johnstown. He divided his force into two divisions, and sent Major Rowley by a circuitous route to fall upon their rear while he engaged them in front. The battle had scarcely begun when the militia broke and fled, nor was Willett able to stop their retreat until they had reached a stone church far in the rear. The enemy were rejoicing over their easy victory and were busy cutting down and scalping stragglers when Major Powley's division fell upon their rear. Another general battle ensued which continued till near dark when Willett succeeded in reorganizing a company to go to the assistance of their companions in arms. The enemy hard pressed on all sides maintained a stubborn resistance till dark when they broke and fled.

The brave colonel remained that night upon the field of battle endeavoring to relieve the sufferings of the wounded. As soon as possible he sent a detachment to Oneida lake to destroy the boats of the enemy, and a scouting party to follow the movements of Ross and Butler. The former failed in their undertaking, but the latter discovered the course of the fleeing army and Willett set out in pursuit. He overtook a small body of them not far from the northern line of the Royal Grant. A sharp fight ensued when some were killed, others taken prisoners, while the remainder fled. The Patriots pressed on in hot pursuit and overtook Butler at Jersey Field, where a short battle was fought resulting in the death of many of the enemy. It was in this battle that an Oneida killed the noted Tory leader, Walter N. Butler, whose body was left in the wilderness without burial. We quote from Stone, "So perished Walter N. Butler, one of the greatest scourges, as he was one of the most fearless men, of his native county. No other event of the whole war created so much joy in the Mohawk valley as the news of his decease."

The death of their leader caused a panic among the enemy and they fled in all directions not occupied by the pursuing Patriots. Night put an end to the pursuit, although it is said that the fleeing Tories did not halt until the following day. Colonel Willett left them to pursue their dreadful march through the snows of a trackless wilderness, nearly 100 miles without food and without blankets, while he returned in triumph with a large number of prisoners and with the loss of but a single man.

# CHAPTER XIX.

## EVENTS SUBSEQUENT TO THE REVOLUTION.

In the treaty of peace in '82 Great Britain made no stipulation in behalf of the Red Men who had so nobly fought for her. Having cast in their fortunes with the side which was vanquished, by the usages of war it would be expected that the conqueror would deprive them of the soil over which they and their fathers had roamed so many years. But Washington and Schuyler both labored with the authorities of New York to give them sections of land on which they might live permanently subject to the general control of the State as they had formerly been under the rule of Great Britain. A meeting of the representatives of the government and of the Six Nations was held at Fort Stanwix where the matter was discussed. Red Jacket, a famous Indian orator and a rival of both Brant and Cornplanter, in an eloquent speech opposed such an arrangement; but Cornplanter clearly foreseeing the folly of striving longer in arms against the Americans, urged the Indians to accept the best terms they could get and be content to live in peace. It was finally agreed that the Iroquois should occupy certain large tracts of land, all of which must lie east of a north and south line running through Buffalo. This treaty caused great dissatisfaction among the Indians, and Red Jacket took this opportunity to draw much of Cornplanter's influence to himself. The latter was rewarded, as will appear later, by the gift of a tract of land on the Alleghany river in Pennsylvania, which was to belong to him and his heirs forever. At the outbreak of the war the English commission had promised, no matter

what the outcome of the war might be, to furnish the
Mohawks with as valuable hunting grounds as they
then possessed. At the close of the war Brant urged their
claims upon the British government and was offered a
large tract of land north of Lake Ontario, but the
Mohawks did not wish to be removed so far from their
confederates, the Senecas, who urged them to settle on
their lands within New York. But inasmuch as they
had cast their fortunes with the English, Brant preferred to have his people live on British soil; so he
succeeded in getting the grant changed to a location
nearer the Senecas. They finally settled on a tract of
land "six miles on each side of the river, from the
mouth to its source," viz: the Ouise or Grand River,
flowing into Lake Erie on the north about 40 miles
from the Falls of Niagara.

Brant at once began to work for the moral and intellectual uplifting of his people. He encouraged the
work of the missionaries and caused portions of the
New Testament to be translated and printed in the
Mohawk language.

At his death he was succeeded by his son John who
with his warriors aided the British in the war of 1812.

We will close this chapter by quoting from the historian Lossing. "From time to time after 1785 the
State and individuals procured lands from the
Indians by cession or by purchase. The Tuscaroras
and Oneidas first parted with some of their territories
in 1785. In 1788 both the Oneidas and the Onondagas disposed of all their lands excepting some reservations, and in 1789 the Cayugas ceded all their lands to
the State, excepting a reservation near Cayuga Lake.
In each case the right of free hunting and fishing in
all the counties was reserved."

"The Senecas parted with most of their territory in
1795. The same year the Mohawks, most of whom

fled to Canada at the close of the war, relinquished all their lands to the State for a consideration. So late as 1819 there were about 5,000 of the Six Nations in the State, in possession, in eleven reservations, of two hundred and seventy-one thousand acres of land. In 1838 these lands had been disposed of, nearly all the titles extinguished, and the Indian population had removed westward across the Mississippi River. Such was the final act in the drama of the once powerful barbarian republic in the State of New York—the great Iroquois League. It has disappeared from the face of the earth and entered the realm of past history."

A few, however, of the different clans remain to preserve the customs and traditions of their fathers. Hemmed in on all sides by the aggressive and grasping Anglo Saxon, they sigh for the departed glory of the days before the white man touched these shores, when their rule extended from the lordly Hudson to the Mississippi, and from the rushing St. Lawrence to the peaceful Carolinas. When we contemplate how quickly this great division of the human family have lost the most beautiful land upon which the sun smiles, how the ploughshare of the invader turns up the bones of their forefathers, their customs and traditions despised, and themselves outcasts and wanderers among a strange people, we are led to exclaim, "Lo the poor Indian!"

# CHAPTER XX.

The following account of the present condition of the Six Nations is taken largely from the Official Census of 1900.

## SAINT REGIS INDIANS

The Saint Regis Indians are the successors of the ancient Mohawks, and their reservation is situated in both St. Lawrence and Franklin counties. They own about 15,000 acres, the greater part of which could easily be made into productive farming land. Some parts are exceptionally fertile and nearly all is well watered. The entire reservation is level or slightly rolling. The timber has been nearly all cut away for fuel. The roads are very poor, in many parts being little more than trails. The Saint Regis Indians also occupy a large tract in Canada, as many, or more, living on English soil as in New York. Three-fourths of the entire tribe are Roman Catholics. They have a pleasant little church, capable of seating 600 people, just across the line on the Canadian border. The Methodists have built a church for the Protestant Indians at a cost of $2,000. The Conference sends a regularly ordained preacher who is supported by the Missionary Society.

Among the Indians that have united with the churches may be found many who are as true to their professions of Christianity as are their white neighbors who have had many more opportunities for religious culture. They are less quarrelsome than many Indians, and are generous, considering the means at their disposal. Intemperance has a strong hold upon many, and especially upon those who are able to wield considerable influence. They are known for the purity of their home life, a condition brought about by the teachings and influence of Christianity. New York maintains 5 separate schools for the education of the children at an annual expense of perhaps $1,500. The cost of the school buildings was about $1,400. The younger generations easily acquire the rudiments of English, but there their education usually stops. The one great drawback in intellectual development is the lack of ability to think and speak in English. One writer has said: "It keeps down the comprehension of ideas, which cannot find expression through the Indian vocabulary, and it is simply impossible for the Indian either to appreciate his condition and needs or make substantial progress until he is compelled by necessity to make habitual use of English."

### THE ONEIDAS

It will be recalled that the Oneidas and the Tuscaroras under the influence of that great and good missionary, Mr. Kirkland, threw in their lot with the Patriots during the Revolution, and it would be supposed that they, after having been so long in sympathy with the civilization of the whites, would have conformed more rapidly to new conditions which grew up after the close of that long and sanguinary strife. But such has not been the case. In 1785 the Tuscaroras united with the Oneidas in selling a large portion of their lands to the State of New York. The tribe kept making treaties with the State and selling more and more of their lands until in 1846 they had but 350 acres left. About this time the greater part of the nation emigrated to Wisconsin leaving a small remnant to hold the land in severalty. There is something pathetic in the thought of these red friends of our forefathers being obliged to see their once happy hunting grounds gradually occupied by the usurping pale face until they were finally compelled to leave the scenes of their youth, and the groves of their fore-fathers by the very people whom they had befriended, and seek new homes far toward the setting sun.

Besides a few scattered families there are two small clusters of houses, one at Orchard near the village of Oneida, and another at Windfall in Madison county. The census of 1890 showed that the children attended no school, and attendance at church was only occasional. The most of them do not till the little land they pretend to own. Much of it is occupied by white people. The Indians work some, by the day, but spend most of their time at such work as basket weaving, or idling about. They are peaceable and some are assimilating with their white neighbors and slowly taking on the manners of civilization. Studying over the present condition of the Oneidas, we were forcibly reminded of the speech of one of their number, "before long there won't be any of us left."

## THE ONONDAGAS

The Onondaga reservation lies in the county of the same name, and is about five miles south of the city of Syracuse. The Indians own about 6100 acres, at least three-fourths of which could be made highly fertile. Underneath the reservation lies a bed of limestone which is quarried for building purposes, and brings in some revenue to the tribe. The greater portion of the farming land is tilled by the whites, some of whom rent of the Indians under sanction of the State. They pay a fair rental which keeps some of the tribe from want. The government is in the hands of twenty-seven chiefs, nearly all of whom belong to the pagan party, and are elected as in olden times by the females of the families represented. In the constitution of 1882 provision was made for a president, judges, clerk, treasurer, marshal, school trustee and other officers. Laws respecting wills, dowers, the settlement of estates and marriage were made to conform more to those of the State of New York.

There are two churches on the reservation, the Protestant Episcopal, and the Methodist. While the number of communicants in each is small, yet the buildings are commodious and would be ornaments to any village. The pastors are earnest and do a good work among the few who profess christianity. The non-christian, or Pagan party, hold their religious rites at the council house of the nation.

If all jealousies and rivalries between the Christian societies could be eliminated, they would wield a greater influence over the Pagan party and eventually might be the means of bringing the tribe to a much higher state of civilization.

The State has provided one school for the Onondaga nation which is held in a building that cost $500. This is centrally located and should be attended by all the children of school age on that reservation. A few, and they are usually the children of Christian Indians, attend regularly, but the greater number are indifferent to education.

### TUSCARORA RESERVATION

This nation occupies a tract of land of about 6200 acres situated in Niagara county five miles from Suspension Bridge. This is one of the best cultivated tracts of all the land owned by the Six Nations. The chiefs compel every land owner to maintain a fence at least four feet high. The larger part of the land is watered with pure springs. The Indians generally till their own land, except those who are physically unable to do manual labor. These lease their farms and live upon the rentals. There are many apple and peach orchards, and the raising of fruit is a source of considerable profit.

Government among the Tuscaroras is administered much as it is among the Onondagas, vacancies among the chiefs being filled by the women of the clans. There are a president, clerk, treasurer, etc.; besides a large number of sachems and chiefs. The laws are few and the people are orderly and peaceable.

The Presbyterians and Baptists both maintain churches each of which has a good Sunday school, good singing, and a fairly intelligent audience. There is also a Ladies' Aid Society in connection with the church.

There are two schools among the Tuscaroras each presided over by competent teachers. The buildings have attractive surroundings, but the attendance is very small.

### THE SENECAS

The Seneca Indians are settled on five different reservations. The Tonawanda, Allegany, Oil Spring, Cornplanter and Cattaraugu .

### TONAWANDA

The Tonawanda reservation embraces about 6,500 acres of land lying partly in each of the counties of Erie, Genesee and Niagara. The roads are poor, and the fences are not well kept up. But little over half of the reservation is cultivated and much of this by white people. A great deal of the timber has been wasted, but there is enough for a few years to come.

There are three church buildings: the Baptist, built of brick at a cost of $3,600, has a membership of forty or fifty. The church members are the proud possessors of a good organ. The Presbyterian church, costing $2,500, is not as large as the first named, nor is it as influential; while the Methodist is the smallest of the three, but perhaps not less active. There are three schools mentioned for the education of these Indians, but little if any more interest is shown in books than by the other Indian nations. By an act of the State Legislature money was set aside to erect and equip a large school for manual training. A farm, teams and implements were provided, but through indifference and mismanagement the whole scheme was dropped and the buildings allowed to go to decay.

The Tonawanda Senecas are governed by thirty-four chiefs elected by the women. The executive officers are elected by a vote of the people.

### ALLEGANY

The Allegany reservation lies in Cattaraugus county and contains over 30,000 acres, of which not much more than 5,000 acres are either under cultivation or used for pasturage. The soil on the uplands is very poor, and the lowlands are subject to floods. A great deal of the land is covered with second growth timber, the former heavy growth having been cut and rafted down the river.

All Allegany and Cattaraugus reservations are both governed by a constitution which provides for the election of a council of sixteen members. There is a president who has the casting vote in case of tie, fills vacancies till the next election, and recommends necessary measures to the council. Also provides for a peacemaker's court elected for three years, which has jurisdiction in all matters relating to wills, estates, real estate and divorces. A clerk, treasurer and marshals are also provided for.

The Presbyterians have one church on this large reservation costing $1500. There are about one hundred members, some of whom labor zealously for the conversion of their tribe. The Baptists have a very small society. The State provides for six schools all of which are indifferently attended.

## OIL SPRING

The Oil Spring reservation contains a small tract of 640 acres. It lies in both Cattaraugus and Allegany counties.

## CORNPLANTER

The Cornplanter reservation lies on both sides of the Alleghany river in Warren county, Pa. It contains nearly 700 acres and is owned by the heirs of the famous chief, Cornplanter. In religious matters these Indians are closely associated with those of the Allegany reservation. The Presbyterians have a small, but well built church with a membership of about forty. They own a church organ and have a good Sunday school.

## CATTARAUGUS

This reservation lies in Cattaraugus, Chautauqua and Erie counties, and contains over 21,000 acres of fertile land mostly in the valley formed by Cattaraugus Creek. The land is well watered and capable of producing large crops. Wood for fuel is scarce, but there are indications of the presence of natural gas which may in the future take the place of that article. The roads are very poor, 'tho some efforts are occasionally made to improve them.

In selecting this spot for their permanent homes, the Senecas exercised good judgment. There are three religious denominations on the reservation. The Methodists have a church which cost nearly $2,000; the Presbyterians have a larger building costing about $2,500; while the Baptist church cost but $1,500. In this as on all the reservations, the Indians pay but little toward the support of the gospel, the greater part of the expenses being paid by some of the organizations of the different churches.

Perhaps the Cattaraugus schools are among the best, if not the best of all the Indian schools. There are ten in number, part of them in charge of experienced teachers. In 1855 Mr. Thomas founded a school which is now known as "The Thomas Orphan Asylum." It has come directly under the control of the State. It has a productive farm, a good boarding home, and hospital, thus making it an ideal home for the orphan children of the Six Nations. There are regular hours for study, recreation and work, and the children are guided by sympathetic and affectionate teachers. The Indian boys and girls display excellent musical talent, and many of them have become really proficient in the common branches, and in physiology, history and drawing. This school clearly demonstrates what might be done to raise the Indian to a higher intellectual plane when he is surrounded by the advantages and opportunities for growth which the more fortunate whites enjoy.

An Iroquois brave at the time of the War of the Revolution, from a painting by
J. Grasset de St. Sauveur.

Misisagas
Torouto

LAKE O

Fort taken from the
French in July 1750.

Great Falls

Ft Sclosser

Small Villages

Canawagus

Chenufsio

Ft
Erie

Part

of Lake

Erie

The Country West and North
of the Boundary Line having
never been surveyed or
even thoughly Explored
is chiefly laid down from
my Journals and the
Sketches of intelligent
Indians and other Persons

SENEC

Ganushago △

Onondarka

Karaghiyadirha

Gistaqu

THE S

Tienienquarante

as it is Called above Ft Pitt

Ohio or Allegany River

Chingleclamoock △

Branch of

△ Kittanning

West

A map of the territory occupied
by the Six Nations Iroquois,
copied from the original manu-
script map in the State Library
in Albany, N.Y.

By the Country of the six Nations proper is meant that part within wh
the rest which is of Vast extent being chiefly occupied by their de
as they reside within the limits of N. York at Fort Hunter & Cent
lies also within that Province the Tuscaroras who form the si
southern People that live on lands allotted them between One

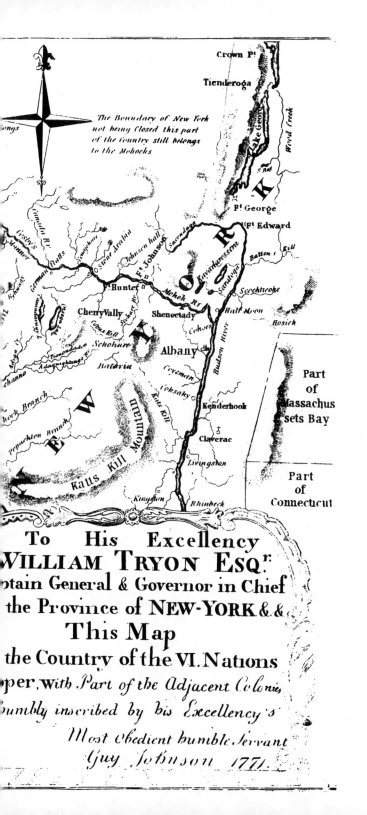

Crown Pt.

Tienderoga

L^e George

The Boundary of New York
not being Closed this part
of the Country still belongs
to the Mohocks

Wood Creek

S. Bay

Ft George

Ft Edward

Y

Canada Rr

Costly's

Stanwix

German Flatts

Carryhorne

Stone Arabia

Johnson hall

F^t Johnson

Sacondaga

Ft Hunter

Mohok Rr.

Kavaderresseva

Batten Kill

Saratoga

Seechticoke

CherryVally

Schoary

Shenectady

Half Moon

Hosick

Schohare

Cohoes

Adaquightingh't

Tionendaroa

Batavia

Albany

Coymau

Kats Kill

Hudson River

Part
of
Massachus
sets Bay

hock Branch

Popachton Branch

Katts Kill Mountain

Coksaky

Kenderhook

Claverac

Livingston

Kingston

Rhinbeck

Part
of
Connecticut

To    His    Excellency
WILLIAM TRYON ESQ^r.
ptain General & Governor in Chief
the Province of NEW-YORK & &
This Map
the Country of the VI. Nations
per, with Part of the Adjacent Colonies
umbly inscribed by his Excellency's
Most Obedient humble Servant
Guy Johnson 1771.